William and Mary

Very Interesting People

*Bite-sized biographies of Britain's most
fascinating historical figures*

William and Mary

Very Interesting People

Tony Claydon
and W. A. Speck

UNIVERSITY PRESS

OXFORD
UNIVERSITY PRESS

Great Clarendon Street, Oxford ox2 6DP

Oxford University Press is a department of the University of Oxford.
It furthers the University's objective of excellence in research, scholarship,
and education by publishing worldwide in

Oxford New York

Auckland Cape Town Dar es Salaam Hong Kong Karachi
Kuala Lumpur Madrid Melbourne Mexico City Nairobi
New Delhi Shanghai Taipei Toronto

With offices in

Argentina Austria Brazil Chile Czech Republic France Greece
Guatemala Hungary Italy Japan Poland Portugal Singapore
South Korea Switzerland Thailand Turkey Ukraine Vietnam

Oxford is a registered trade mark of Oxford University Press
in the UK and in certain other countries

Published in the United States
by Oxford University Press Inc., New York

First published in the *Oxford Dictionary of National Biography* 2004
This paperback edition first published 2007

© Oxford University Press 2007

Database right Oxford University Press (maker)

First published 2007

British Library Cataloguing in Publication Data

Data available

Library of Congress Cataloging in Publication Data

Data available

Typeset by SPI Publisher Services, Pondicherry, India
Printed in Great Britain
on acid-free paper by
Ashford Colour Press Ltd, Gosport, Hampshire

ISBN 978–0–19–921754–0 (Pbk.)

10 9 8 7 6 5 4 3 2 1

Contents

Preface

William and Mary are perhaps the most under-rated British monarchs. Outside Northern Ireland (where William has became a—somewhat paradoxical—symbol of protestant resistance), the king has been largely forgotten by the general public, while Mary—if recognized at all—is known only as a constitutionally curious adjunct to her husband. Yet this royal pair ruled at a period of political transformation, and they were crucial to its surprising success.

When William invaded England in 1688 he ended an experiment in English absolutism by his father-in-law, James II, which many contemporaries feared would become as complete as that of Louis XIV in France. He subsequently presided as Westminster politicians invented a new style of parliamentary polity; and while his suppression of Highland clans and Irish Catholics complicated relations between England, Scotland and Ireland, his decision to take these nations into his lifelong struggle with the French laid foundations in military logistics, bureaucratic organization, and public finance which later allowed the United Kingdom to emerge as the world's premier power. The queen, meanwhile facilitated her husband's work. She governed at home while he led his armies abroad, and she proved adept at the sort of public relations needed to win support for a controversial new regime. One might even argue she helped invent modern monarchy. Under these rulers, crowned heads began to lead more through dedicated public service and moral example than direct exercise of prerogative: Mary, with her stress on visible virtue at court and her pious dedication to God and country, did at least as much as her husband to introduce this style. Given these achievements, and the undeserved obscurity into which William and Mary have subsequently fallen, we are delighted that these biographies have appeared together in a concise and accessible volume. We hope this will help to revive the fame of these figures, and lead to better appreciation of their significance.

Along with the other titles in this series, the lives were originally produced as entries for the *Oxford Dictionary of National Biography* (2004). Our brief in writing them was to introduce their subjects to the general reader, while providing a context which would allow wider understanding of their age. As this is the purpose of this current publication also, we have decided to reproduce them virtually as they first appeared. We also decided against major revision because the original articles seemed to work so well together. Although they were written individually, with only minimal consultation between the authors, the close interdependence of William and Mary's lives ensured the two essays had much to say to one another, and our common curiosity about how the post-1688 regime survived its extraordinary birth provided further shared themes. Of course, advances in scholarship sometimes demand that work be updated: but here we have actually benefited from the traditional neglect of our subjects. Although a fine group of researchers has worked on the later Stuarts in the past few decades, and although we profited hugely from their works as we wrote, William and Mary have never been debated and interrogated as closely as, say, Henry VIII, Elizabeth or Charles I. As a result, the pace of historiographic change is not exhausting, and we think our broad conclusions can stand.

One possible exception is the reading of politics in the Netherlands in the biography on William. Recent work by Dutch researchers suggests his 'Orange party' was a much looser alliance than is argued in this volume, and that his reported purge of opponents in the 1670s could not have been systematic or William would have forfeited the vital support of local élites. These findings are very well expressed in Wout Troost's excellent *William III: the Stadholder-King* (2005), and we thank that author for his careful reading of the Dutch sections of this piece. Curious readers can weigh the new interpretations in Troost's book, but in fact they are not so very distant from the lessons emphasized here. Whatever its precise structure, so much Dutch government was outside William's direct control, that even if he had hoped he could command it without negotiation and compromise, he would soon be disabused. For the queen, Maureen Waller's well documented *Ungrateful Daughters: the Stuart Princesses who Stole their Father's Crown* (2002) clearly goes against the favourable view presented here, but we persist with a positive (though not entirely conventional) conclusion. William and Mary succeeded because they showed skills of presentation, persuasion, and consensus-building which had been notably lacking in their Stuart predecessors. As we show, however, they honed these skills during their time in the Netherlands. It is therefore possible that England—if not Britain—was set on a path to greatness by the example of a foreign republic. Perhaps it has been reluctance to recognize this which has led William and Mary to be forgotten.

Tony Claydon and W.A. Speck
January 2007

About the authors

Tony Claydon is Senior Lecturer in History at the University of Wales Bangor. He is interested in religion and political culture in the century after the Restoration in England and is author of *William III and the Godly Revolution* (1996), *William III* ('Profiles in Power', 2002), and *Europe and the Making of England, 1660–1760* (2007).

W. A. Speck is Emeritus Professor of History at Leeds University and currently Special Professor in the School of English at Nottingham University. His publications include *Reluctant Revolutionaries: Englishmen and the Revolution of 1688* (1988) and *James II* ('Profiles in Power', 2002). His latest book is *Robert Southey: Entire Man of Letters* (2006).

Abbreviations

NS   'New Style', the name given to the dates of the
Gregorian calendar used in continental Europe, and
eleven days ahead of the Julian calendar used in
Britain until 1752

OS   'Old Style', the name given to the dates of the Julian
calendar used in Britain until 1752 and eleven days
behind the Gregorian calendar

William

by Tony Claydon

The triumph of Orangism

1

William III and II (1650–1702),
king of England, Scotland, and Ireland, and prince of
Orange, was born in the Binnenhof Palace in The Hague
on 14 November 1650 NS. He was the posthumous and only
child of William II, prince of Orange (1626–1650), who had
died from smallpox eight days before he was born, and of his
consort, Mary (1631–1660), eldest daughter of Charles I and
princess royal of England. He was baptized Willem Hendrik
(William Henry) on 15 January 1651 NS.

Family circumstances and dynastic fortunes

Despite the republican constitution of the United Provinces,
William was destined from birth to play a central role in
Dutch politics. It is true that the sovereign power in the
Netherlands was not William's family, but rather the states
(or governing assemblies) of the constituent provinces, along
with the federal states general, which contained representatives from these bodies. It is also true that these assemblies
were dominated by a regent oligarchy of town magistrates or

burgomeesters, and that traditions of unanimity made it difficult for any one person to dictate policy. Notwithstanding this, however, William's ancestors had built up such a pre-eminent position in the Low Countries that they enjoyed a quasi-monarchical status.

The roots of this dominance lay in the Dutch revolt. The Orange family's leadership of the long struggle for independence from Spain had given it a charismatic reputation as the founder of the nation, which in turn had brought an almost automatic claim on the office of stadholder in most of the provinces. This post, a remnant from the days of the Spanish viceroys, carried with it a package of useful powers, including the right to choose burgomeesters from lists submitted by the municipalities. Other traditional appointments as admiral and as captain-general brought further influence. They bestowed control of the federal armed forces, and added to the networks of patronage which helped build an Orange 'party' in Dutch politics. To these advantages were added the riches of the family (it owned extensive estates both within the territories of the republic and outside in Flanders, Burgundy, and Germany); the prestige which came with the hereditary sovereignty of the principality of Orange in southern France; and the recently concluded alliance with British royalty. The stadholders had also surrounded themselves with a rich ceremonial life which allowed them to represent what a contemporary called 'the Dignity of [the] State' (Temple, 73). In theory, therefore, the infant William was guaranteed a life of considerable power.

Unfortunately for the young prince, events in the years immediately before William's birth had brought his family to one of its lowest ebbs. Extravagance had run up debts; the English regicide of 1649 meant that no Stuart support was forthcoming; and the following year William II's attempt to coerce the province of Holland into paying for larger armed forces had backfired. The city of Amsterdam had resisted the Orange army, and public sympathy had deserted a stadholder seen to have attempted a *coup d'état*. The sudden death of William's father therefore struck a dynasty already weakened. Worse still, the prince's demise left the family with no adult male head and divided in battle for guardianship of his son between the deceased's widow and his mother, the dowager Princess Amalia. Although an agreement of 13 August 1651 NS made Mary guardian, with Amalia and her son-in-law the elector of Brandenburg co-guardians, this formal settlement did not prevent repeated squabbles. Taking advantage of these divisions, a 'republican' alignment organized to take control of Dutch policy. Centring its strength on Amsterdam, this group was co-ordinated by Johann de Witt, the grand pensionary of Holland, and worked steadily to limit Orange power for the next two decades. William's early years were therefore dictated by struggles to overcome the débâcles surrounding his birth.

The Orange party began its bid for power in dramatic fashion at William's baptism. For the service in the Groote Kerk in The Hague the prince was dressed in regal ermine, and was accompanied by a ceremonial guard as if he were already stadholder. At the same time his mother and his grandmother wrote separately to provincial states reminding them of William's claims on public offices. Sadly for him, however, the republicans were already mobilizing, and the ill co-ordinated correspondence from the competing leaders of the Orange cause merely demonstrated their incompetence. Within days of William II's death the states of Holland had decided to leave its own stadholdership indefinitely vacant, and put successful pressure on neighbouring Zeeland to do the same. At a 'great assembly' of all provinces, which opened in January 1651, the republicans dissuaded the provinces of Utrecht, Gelderland, and Overijssel from filling their own stadholderships, and suspended the captain-generalship. Taken together, these measures represented an anti-Orangist constitutional revolution. The posts the prince would normally have inherited were effectively abolished. Worse was to follow. In 1654 peace negotiations to end the First Anglo-Dutch War included pressure from Oliver Cromwell—in collusion with de Witt—for a permanent bar on the house of Orange from its traditional offices. This resulted in an act of exclusion by which Holland agreed never to appoint William stadholder.

Signs of any Orangist revival among these defeats were scant. There were substantial Orange forces outside Holland, and opposition from these prevented the 1654 exclusion applying beyond that province. Also, William's uncle Frederick William, stadholder of Friesland and Gronigen, promoted the young prince's cause throughout the 1650s—albeit in hopes of dominating the infant. Yet little came of this support, since the sympathetic provinces were badly divided among themselves. There were some glimmerings of hope in 1660 when William's uncle Charles II (1630–1685) was restored to the English throne. At this point Holland's urban élites saw trading opportunities in improved relations with the Stuarts and sought to placate the new king by removing his nephew's legal disabilities. Zeeland, three inland provinces, and even some towns in Holland pressed for William to be granted the usual 'high charges' when he reached maturity (Israel, *Dutch Republic*, 751). De Witt was consequently forced to accept both repeal of the 1654 exclusion and negotiations with Mary Stuart. These ended with the prince's being adopted by the states general as a 'child of state', being granted an allowance out of government funds, and being educated in preparation for an undefined, but major, political role. Despite these setbacks, however, republicans were soon back in charge. Mary Stuart's death in January 1661 NS (December 1660 OS)—and more especially her will, which bestowed the guardianship of William back on Amalia—destroyed the child of state deal and so excused de Witt from having to raise a potential rival. Meanwhile, Dutch élites were disappointed by the new British monarch's hostility to their commercial interests and lost enthusiasm for his family. By September 1662 de Witt had secured agreement from the states of Holland and Zeeland that they would accept no promotion of William until he was eighteen.

A second revival of Orangism in the difficult early months of the Second Anglo-Dutch War was similarly short-lived. Over the winter of 1665–6 de Witt faced popular demonstrations in favour of Prince William and absurd demands that the militarily inexperienced fifteen-year-old be made captain-general. Once again, however, the republican grouping soon regained control as naval victories resolidified support. By April 1666 de Witt had the political strength to move in on William's household. In return for granting the prince a pension, he sacked servants who he correctly believed had been co-ordinating Orangist agitation, and took charge of the prince's education. The triumph was completed over the next eighteen months. By 2 August 1667 NS de Witt had secured the 'perpetual edict ... for the preservation of freedom' in the states of Holland. This abolished the provincial stadholdership and committed Holland to rejecting any captain-general who was stadholder anywhere else. In January 1668 four out of the seven provinces accepted a 'harmony' which, while it assigned William a place on the advisory council of state and promised that he would eventually be considered for captain-general, also barred the prince from stadholderships and declared he would be ineligible for either council or captaincy until he had reached twenty-three.

William's education

In all these machinations William himself was too young to play much part. The prince had, in fact, been allowed a remarkably private early life, only marginally affected by the political storms which swirled around his schoolroom. Until he was three the child lived in his mother's household in the Binnenhof apartments. After this he was granted his own establishment in the same building, while Mary began spending long periods away with her exiled brother, the future Charles II. William's education began in 1656 under a Hague divine, Cornelius Trigland, and was put on a more formal basis in 1659 when a governor was appointed (Frederick of Nassau, heer van Zuylestein—a dashing but conspiratorial cavalry officer) and when the household moved to Leiden so that the prince could be instructed by the university faculty.

The collapse of the child of state scheme in 1661 meant that these arrangements were not affected. William therefore continued an education which ultimately proved better at imbuing a solid Calvinism, a sense of Orange historical destiny, and a passion for hunting, than affability. More disturbing for William was the republican storming of his household in 1666. The prince begged to retain Zuylestein, to whom he had become devoted, but de Witt insisted the governor be replaced and himself began to spend many hours with the boy. During these conferences de Witt tried to instil both a love of Dutch freedoms and a training in political tactics. William's later disregard for the republican constitution suggests he had little success with the first project—but De Witt did impress with his integrity, and his practice of setting practical political conundrums as educational exercises was useful. William certainly praised the pensionary when asked about him in later years, telling Gilbert Burnet that his teacher had been 'one of the greatest men of the age' (*Bishop Burnet's History*, ed. Burnet and Burnet, 1.321). In admitting this the prince must have been aware of an irony. De Witt had groomed a child who would soon play the major part in his destruction.

Coming to power, 1668–1672

During his youth William's personal involvement in politics had been limited to occasional public appearances. Yet from 1668, as the balance of political power within the United Provinces began to shift, William started to take an active role in the recovery of his position. The essential background here was the weakening of de Witt. This was partly the result of resentment at the pensionary's long dominance.

Regents in Holland who felt excluded from power began to think more seriously about collaboration with the house of Orange. More importantly, however, de Witt lost power as a result of deteriorating relations with France. From the late 1660s it became clear that Louis XIV was intent on absorbing the strategically vital Spanish Netherlands and other border lands, and de Witt's inability to counter this threat set the Dutch searching for an alternative saviour.

William's most significant early action was to travel to Middelburg on 19 September 1668 NS to accept the honour of 'first noble of the states of Zeeland'. Taken under the pretext of a hunting trip, this promotion to a traditional Orange office brought the prince effective control of the province and, perhaps more importantly, provided a symbolic opportunity to claim leadership of the entire republic. An English observer, Edward Browne, recorded the near-regal entertainments provided for the prince in Zeeland (British Library, Sloane MS 1908, fol. 19). Acceptance of the first nobleship also signalled William's majority. On 25 October Amalia ended her guardianship and handed over control of the Orange estates. From this point, William pushed hard to secure his inheritance. Building on support in the inland provinces, mobilizing his new power in Zeeland, and forming an alliance with those in Holland willing to work with him, he campaigned for immediate admission to the council of state. Despite de Witt's claims that he could not be of age until 1673, the new political alignment carried the issue. On 31 May 1670 NS William went on to the council with the house of Orange's traditional concluding vote. Forging onward, and hoping to gain from the old Dutch tendency to look to his house in times of

foreign threat, the prince pressed to be made admiral and
captain-general. De Witt argued that promotion would vio-
late the legal barriers to Orange promotion that he had put
in place, but the Williamite current proved too powerful. By
the meeting of the states general in 1672 all the provinces
but Holland had agreed to promote him to the federal military offices. On 24 February even Holland's will collapsed
after William had refused its proposal for a temporary post,
and as it became increasingly clear that Louis XIV planned a
wholesale invasion of the United Provinces in alliance with
England and the bishops of Münster and Cologne.

By early spring 1672 only the lack of stadholderships stood
between William and his ancient family dignity. At this
point, however, two things delayed any campaign to recover
these. First, William had sworn not to seek these offices
under the perpetual edict, and was too mindful of his honour
(and of the effect on popular opinion) to break this oath.
Second, and more importantly, France's war preparations
had to be countered. Unless some response could be found to
Louis XIV's threat, there would be no United Provinces left
to lead. William therefore spent the spring concentrating
on the duties of captain-general rather than campaigns for
further promotion. The task facing the new commander
was daunting. William had to make frantic efforts to bol-
ster an army weakened by twenty years of inaction under
de Witt, and in particular had to arrange for emergency
defences along the Ijssel, since it had become evident Louis
would bypass the protecting Habsburg army in the Spanish
Netherlands and invade eastwards from Münster. By the
time William went to the army camp on 19 April NS, it was
clear that the republic was in trouble, and what he found

in the field was truly horrifying. The forces were seriously under strength at only 8000 troops, and were badly under-equipped. Despite vigorous efforts William was reporting by mid-May that he doubted he could hold the Ijssel. His fears were justified. When hostilities started in earnest in June, Dutch defences dissolved. Troops from Münster and Cologne occupied large parts of Gelderland, Groningen, and Overijssel, while the French crossed the Rhine and took town after town before capturing Utrecht on 27 June NS. By the end of the month, therefore, the Dutch were left with little of their country but Friesland in the far north-west, and Holland and Zeeland, which were only saved by flooding the land between them and the French forces.

In other circumstances such a débâcle would have ended the ambitions of a captain-general. In William's case, how-ever, the reverse was true. Within weeks he had attained an unprecedented dominance in the Netherlands. There were three main reasons for this. First, de Witt was the easiest person to blame for the disaster: his diplomacy had failed to contain Louis XIV, and his neglect of the army had weakened the state's defences. Secondly, although William's early refusal to withdraw his army was questionable, his determination was not, and his heroic defiance of Louis earned popular adulation. He worked night and day to find troops to man vital points of defence, and he initially refused to abandon the line of the Ijssel, stating that if the French crossed the river the Dutch should 'believe that I am dead' (Rowen, 830). Thirdly, William was aided by a vast outpouring of propaganda. As the French advanced

Orangists let loose a torrent of invective blaming de Witt for the country's peril and assuring audiences that only their captain-general could save them.

The effects of these forces were soon evident. As the other provinces fell, pro-Orange demonstrations erupted across Holland and Zeeland. At Dordrecht riots against republican party magistrates became so bad by late June that the town's leaders feared total loss of control. In desperation they sent for William, telling him that anarchy would ensue if he did not come to the town to quell the mob. When he arrived, on 29 June NS, he was faced by a crowd demanding that he be declared stadholder. Despite William's initial attempts to ignore the suggestion, mobs trapped him in an inn until the magistrates had formally called for his elevation. The prince returned to his camp that evening, still not having accepted promotion, but the movement to have him declared stadholder was now unstoppable. Councils in Rotterdam, Haarlem, and Gouda were forced to repeat Dordrecht's actions by the end of the 29th and disturbances pulled other cities into line over the next days. Zeeland made William stadholder on 2 July NS; the next day the states of Holland set aside its (now not so) perpetual edict, and proclaimed the prince its stadholder too. After confirmation that he was now absolved from his oaths, William accepted the office in a ceremony in The Hague on 9 July NS. Nor did this end the tidal wave of Orangism. Continuing unrest forced the resignation of republican party magistrates across Holland and Zeeland, and on 20 August NS, in a mercifully rare act of actual violence, de Witt was lynched, murdered, and mutilated. Although William was visibly appalled by this last action, and although he had been careful throughout the summer to avoid seeming to promote his own cause (even staying silent at the Hague festivities), the prince had equally failed to defend de Witt, and had allowed mobs to deliver everything for which he might have hoped.

Stadholder, 1672–1688

William's power in the Netherlands

William's objective from 1672 to his death can be stated very simply. Fired by his personal resentment at France's steady occupation of family lands, and by a deep commitment to a Europe composed of independent nations, the prince's prime aim was to contain Louis XIV. In part this policy involved bringing as many other powers as possible into conflict with France. Ultimately this would lead William to intervene in England in 1688, but before then his chief task was to preserve Dutch commitment to war. His success in this aim was finely balanced. The events of 1672 had given the prince considerable power in the United Provinces, but opposition soon revived, and for long periods proved strong enough to frustrate him.

William's advantages stemmed partly from the formal powers of his offices. As stadholder of provinces he enjoyed the traditional influence over municipal appointments, and also gained the emergency power of *wetsverzettingen*— the right to purge town administrations—which he used extensively. Appointment as admiral and captain-general gave the prince military force, while special powers granted under the *regeringsreglement* gave him the right to reconstitute government in Utrecht, Gelderland, and Overijssel as these provinces were freed from occupation. Beyond this technical authority of office William enjoyed informal advantages. For example, extensive patronage and the continued existence of an Orange party allowed him to bypass some of the rigid mechanisms of Dutch government. Especially in the early years of his rule, aristocratic allies such as Everard van Dijkvelt and Hans Willem Bentinck were given *ad hoc* commissions in administration and diplomacy, and displaced the regent-bureaucrats who had previously run the state. The support of Gaspar Fagel, a one-time ally of de Witt, was similarly crucial. As the new grand pensionary, he controlled debates in the states of Holland and was the head of the Dutch civil service. Added to all this was an impressive ideological power. William magnified his charisma through an efficiently organized propaganda machine. Centred on Fagel, this gathered information from across Europe, used a variety of pamphleteers and engravers to craft it into publicity material, and then took advantage of the unrivalled Dutch printing industry to mass produce its product.

Taken together William's sources of influence were impressive, but the new stadholder still faced considerable obstacles. Most importantly, there was Amsterdam. The magistrates of this city were largely independent of William since—almost uniquely—the stadholder did not have the power to appoint the burgomeesters in this town. Worse, the city fathers soon became unenthusiastic about the war with France. Amsterdam made its money from international

trade, which was disrupted by fighting, and was liable to
pay a substantial proportion of the nation's wartime taxation because the republic's wealth was concentrated among
its citizens. The town therefore tended to lead resistance
to prolonged conflict and, unfortunately for William, was
effectively the paymaster of the state. As William's conflict
dragged on, war weariness ensured that the problems with
Amsterdam spread elsewhere. Within a very few years of
1672 regents across the nation were becoming less enthusiastic for conflict, and the stadholder found even the magistrates he had put in place turned against his policy. Reluctant to endanger further support by purging again, William
found his early dominance evaporating.

War and peace

At first, of course, William had little problem. In 1672 the
threat to the very survival of the republic solidified sentiment around its new leader and the prince was able to
lead his people in defiance of France. Over the summer
he rejected English and French peace terms, telling the
English ambassadors that the best way to avoid seeing his
country lost was to die in the last ditch (*Bishop Burnet's
History*, ed. Burnet and Burnet, 1.327). Instead of capitu-
lating he put his faith in flooded fields and built up his
army—both increasing its numbers to 30,000 men and
reinstilling discipline through high-profile, and sometimes
brutal, courts martial. By the autumn he felt strong enough
to lead an expedition to Maastricht and Charleroi. While
this did not capture any towns, it did give the young commander vital first experience, and allowed him to demon-
strate a formidable—if not reckless—personal courage. It

also forced the French to draw some of their troops away from the front line. By December, therefore, the Dutch could begin to look upon the prince as the providential, perhaps even apocalyptic, saviour of the fatherland which his propaganda styled him.

The next couple of years saw a similar pattern of William's maintaining support and even beginning to enjoy victories. Although Maastricht was lost in June 1673, the prince landed his first major punch in September with the capture of Naarden, and in November joined troops from his newly secured allies of Spain and Austria in a daring attack on Bonn. Although this last action took the Dutch well outside their own territory, it drew the French out of the Netherlands as well, and meant that by the end of the year they held only isolated towns inside the United Provinces' borders. Meanwhile naval defeats forced the English out of the contest (February 1674), and two months later the bishop of Münster was brought to make peace, with the result that Gelderland and Overijssel were freed. October 1674 saw William's eviction of the French from Grave, a success which partly compensated for the bloody draw at Seneffe (11 August NS) and the bungling failure to take Oudenarde later that month.

Initially such success strengthened William's domestic position. He had gained the stadholdership of Utrecht when that province was evacuated by the French, and continuing victories brought further elevation. In February 1674 Fagel took up the town of Haarlem's suggestion that the stadholdership of Holland be made hereditary in William's male line, and successfully piloted it through the states.

Zeeland and Utrecht soon followed suit. In 1675 William was made stadholder of liberated Overijssel, and on 20 April NS the federal military offices were made hereditary as well. These promotions, however, represented the high water mark of the prince's advance. Paradoxically, while armed victory bolstered his reputation, it also gave the Dutch a security which allowed criticism of the prince's more high-handed behaviour. By 1674 the first signs of the new mood began to show. When liberated Gelderland proposed that William be made, not its stadholder, but rather its sovereign duke, reaction elsewhere was hostile. Fears were expressed that ducal status would be an attack on the free constitution of the whole Netherlands. Republican propaganda flowed; three of the six voting towns in Zeeland objected to William's promotion and in Holland normally pro-Orange cities such as Leiden and Haarlem joined Amsterdam in vigorous protest. As a result William was forced to back down. On meeting the states of Gelderland on 20 February 1675 NS the prince rejected the dukedom, satisfying himself with the stadholdership and purges of hostile magistrates. From here his popular support declined. Pamphlets criticized the cost of the war, the trade slump it had produced, and the prince's military adventures outside the provinces. Above all they attacked the corruption of the Orange party and William's use of prerogative, patronage, and purge to smother opposition. By 1677 fear of his ambition was rife and anti-Williamite Amsterdam was making the political running.

Sadly William had little military triumph to compensate for these political troubles. The 1675 campaigning season passed almost without incident and he failed to impress in the next three years of struggle. In May 1676 he managed to outface the French army at Valenciennes without battle, but then failed to take Maastricht in a badly organized seven-week siege. Early next spring the French took Valenciennes, and then inflicted a heavy defeat on the captain-general at Mont Cassel as he marched to relieve St Omer. William failed to draw the French out into open battle at Charleroi in July, and ended the season with only the insignificant capture of Binch. When the French made significant gains in the early months of 1678 the mood in the Netherlands became noticeably anti-war, and Louis cashed in by appealing to the regent class over the stadholder's head. When France offered tariff concessions and preservation of the United Provinces' pre-conflict borders as a basis for a peace treaty, the élites of Holland's towns were won over, and Amsterdam secured a vote in the states general to cease hostilities in June. Louis nearly handed victory back to William by refusing to evacuate towns he had agreed to return but, seeing the Dutch prepared to rejoin the war, he returned to the first deal and concluded the treaty of Nijmegen on 10 August NS. Four days later William managed to use lack of confirmation of the treaty as an excuse to attack French lines at Mons, but the vicious and inconclusive battle which resulted could not hide the fact that he had lost an important round of his domestic struggle.

The Nijmegen peace was a shock for William, but it does appear to have stimulated a re-evaluation of political tactics which ultimately led to greater success. After the treaty he gradually abandoned attempts to bulldoze or outflank the peace party, and instead conciliated its members. Thus over 1679 and 1680 William permitted the rehabilitation of many of the regents who had been expelled in his purges after 1672, and admitted to the poor quality of some he had appointed. The fruits of the new approach were soon evident. Late in 1679 the stadholder persuaded the states general to reject Louis's offer of a treaty, pointing out it was a cover for further encroachments along France's borders. In 1681 the states general confirmed an alliance William had negotiated with Sweden; and in a speech of 7 March 1682 the prince convinced the Dutch they must send 8000 troops to Luxembourg to persuade the French to lift a blockade of the city.

1683 saw another agreement to send troops to challenge Louis, this time in the Spanish Netherlands, but the year also saw a temporary return to the old pattern of William's arousing opposition as he tried to browbeat his opponents. In the late autumn he proposed that the United Provinces raise 16,000 men to deal with any further strong-arm tactics by the French. Amsterdam objected, arguing that troops would be expensive and would provoke Louis needlessly. William's reaction was to hurl all his power at the city. In November he led a delegation from towns which approved an expansion of the army to Amsterdam, making a full ceremonial entry into the town. In January 1684 Fagel argued that decisions to raise troops did not have to be unanimous in the states of Holland (effectively removing the chief city's veto), and on 16 February NS the prince himself presented evidence that Amsterdam's magistrates had been in treasonous correspondence with France.

Reaction to all this was instant and disastrous. Neither magistrates nor crowd were overawed by William's visit to Amsterdam: instead dark comparisons were made with his father's coup attempt in 1650 and mob hostility forced the prince to withdraw. Meanwhile Amsterdam's delegates protested against Fagel's interpretation of Holland's constitution in the states, and simply walked out when accused of treason, effectively blocking any further business. By spring 1684 it was clear the city had won. Few troops could be raised if Amsterdam would not pay for them, and peace-party propaganda swayed Dutch opinion. On 13 May NS the states of Holland passed a resolution forbidding its troops to travel to the Spanish Netherlands. The United Provinces did nothing when Louis besieged and took Luxembourg in May, and on 16 June NS they accepted a twenty-year truce from the French in return for their acquiescence in Louis's recent gains. This last deal was a particularly bitter blow for William, forcing him to accept the loss of family estates in Chiny and St Vith, and France's effective annexation of his ancient patrimony of Orange.

Thus by spring 1684 William was back where he had been six years earlier. He had lost the political battle and faced a nation wholly unwilling to contain Louis. Once again, however, defeat taught the prince valuable lessons, and he returned with still more determination to conciliation. It has been said that he never again attempted any action without having squared Amsterdam first (Israel, *Dutch Republic*, 836). Certainly attempts to improve relations followed hard on the débâcle of 1683–4. Over the next winter the stadholder made contact with the more moderate of the Amsterdam burgomeesters and built up a party of potential supporters. When it became clear William could not secure a large army he reacted calmly, and spoke in favour of Amsterdam's alternative suggestion that foreign threats could be contained by a strong navy. Elsewhere William balanced Orange supporters with members of the peace party in magisterial appointments, and reassured the Dutch he was not seeking to break controls on his power. Thus, although William was still a long way from persuading his nation back to war with France in the years 1686 and 1687, he was slowly dispelling its suspicion. The reward for this would come in 1688, when the states general gave unprecedented backing to his invasion of England.

Britain: diplomacy and marriage

The key to understanding William's intervention in Britain is to review his interaction with the Stuart realm over the preceding two decades. The central influence upon this was, of course, the prince's parentage. The fact that his mother was sister to both Charles II and to James II (1633–1701) meant that he was an integral part of the ruling dynasty. Such clan ties could have produced a close relationship between Britain and the United Provinces. In fact, the connections produced only tension, with both sides wanting to exploit the other. The British kings wished to use their nephew for two main purposes. First, they hoped William would help their foreign policy. Attempting to dominate their young kinsman, Charles and James tried to moderate the United Provinces' hostility to France and so avoid a war in which they must either support Louis (and risk domestic anger at an alliance with an ambitious Catholic power) or support the Dutch (and alienate a Bourbon monarchy which backed them financially). Secondly, the English kings wished to employ the prince as a weapon in domestic

politics. Since their main problem in Britain was their subjects' suspicion of their sympathies with popery, it was useful
to parade a staunchly protestant relative at moments of
crisis. In response to these attempts to use him William in
turn tried to use his uncles to help him contain France. He
would try to help Charles and James in domestic affairs,
but only to unite the British in hostility to Versailles; and
although he tried to co-ordinate his foreign policy with
his uncles, he undermined them whenever they favoured
Louis. With such contradictory objectives, relations within
the Stuart clan were set. Constant expressions of family
affection in correspondence threw only a thin veil over suspicions which culminated in the rupture of 1688.

William's first close contact with his uncles occurred during
a visit to England over the winter of 1670–71. It was
inauspicious. The prince disgraced himself when forced to
'drink very hard' at court, and formed an abiding disgust at
Charles's lack of religious or political principles (*Memoirs
of Sir John Reresby*, 82). During this visit, Gilbert Burnet
claimed, William became convinced his uncle would never
give him 'any real assistance' (*Bishop Burnet's History*, ed.
Burnet and Burnet, 1.501–2). If that was the prince's opinion,
it was dramatically confirmed in 1672. Then Charles joined
France's attack on the Dutch republic, and tried to benefit from the elevation of his nephew which this invasion
produced. Once William was stadholder Charles bombarded
him with patronizing letters, urging him to accept a quick
peace with Louis. Under the proposed deal the Dutch would
lose large tracts of territory, but the prince would be promoted to a power which his 'forefathers always aimed at'
(Bryant, 257). This was a clear attempt to bribe William into

accepting British policy, using sovereignty over the rump of the provinces as bait. The prince, however, was unmoved. Astonished at Charles's opportunism, and full of patriotic faith that the Dutch would fight harder 'preserving their liberty, than for any prince', he sent the king's negotiators away disappointed (*Bishop Burnet's History*, ed. Burnet and Burnet, 1.598). Relations worsened over 1673 as the Dutch navy humiliated the English, and as William used his propaganda machine to stir up anti-court sentiment in the Westminster parliament. Charles was rankled by the treaty of 1674 which forced him out of the war, and he spent much of the 1670s pestering his nephew to accept English mediation between the provinces and France.

There was a temporary thaw in Anglo-Dutch relations in the later 1670s. However, this was largely because Charles was forced to surrender control of policy to the fiercely anti-French Thomas Osborne, earl of Danby, the only man who could control parliament and defend the court against growing popular hostility. The most significant effect of the thaw was William's marriage to James's elder daughter, Mary (1662–1694; later Mary II). This ceremony (the result of the extensive negotiations outlined in the later chapters on Mary) took place in Whitehall on the prince's twenty-seventh birthday, 4 November 1677; and obviously strengthened William's involvement in British politics. The personal aspects of this wedding are also described later. Here it is important to note that, despite general Stuart satisfaction with the match—Charles reputedly encouraged the prince on his wedding night with cries of 'Now, nephew to your work! hey! St George and England!' (Hutton, 346)—the marriage did not break the pattern of clan cross-purposes.

William hoped marrying Mary would involve England in the war with France; Charles and James hoped the match would dispel popular antipathy to their court and provide a new lever on the prince.

Worsening relations, 1678–1685

Just how little progress had really been made in relations became apparent in the years of the exclusion crisis in England. This series of events began late in 1678 with rumours of a popish plot to assassinate Charles. In the uproar that followed Danby was implicated and swept from power. This was a disaster for William. He lost his firmest ally in England and could only respond with a letter assuring the earl that he believed none of the accusations made against him. Even greater challenges followed. Anti-popish hysteria led to demands in parliament that the openly Catholic James be excluded from inheriting the throne. Although the exclusion of James could bring the prince control of British foreign policy (since it might mean the crown's passing to his wife), it also posed dangers for William. If he appeared ambitious to use Mary to achieve royal status he might forfeit Dutch support, and he could be wrong-footed in British politics if he became associated with the pro-exclusionist whig party before they were certain of victory. William also knew he would have to handle relations with his uncles carefully. Still wanting an anti-French alliance, he could not alienate his relatives by suggesting their monarchy be remodelled, and he anyway had a Stuart's reluctance to see this happen. Equally, however, William wanted Charles and James to negotiate with their legislature. The prince knew that England could not be a counterweight to Louis unless the court had the backing of the purse-carrying parliament, and was therefore desperate to avoid a political rupture.

William's response to this web of demands was extreme caution. He refused to go over to England in the early summer of 1679 when James thought this would pacify public opinion and cause demands for his disqualification to fade. Similarly, however, he repeatedly refused to visit London in 1680, when supporters of exclusion thought parading a protestant heir might help their cause. The prince entertained James in The Hague in March and April 1679 when the king sent his brother abroad out of harm's way, but in the autumn of that year showed similar hospitality to Charles's illegitimate son, James Scott, duke of Monmouth, who was being canvassed as a possible protestant alternative to James. Over the next twelve months William formally opposed constitutional changes, but collected information as Charles's court vacillated between trying to face down exclusion, considering accepting it, allowing James to succeed but putting constitutional limitations on him, and appointing William regent for his uncle. By the autumn of 1680, however, the prince had begun to feel he must come off the fence. Realizing that parliamentary demands for exclusion were strengthening, he decided acceptance of an exclusion bill was the only way to get monarchy and legislature working together. He accordingly denounced the alternative of constitutional limitations, stating they would be 'prejudicial to all the royal family', and suggested to Henry Sidney he would go to England to campaign for exclusion if Charles opted for that solution (*Diary of…Sidney*, 2.139, 148).

Disastrously, William's moves in favour of exclusion came just as Charles had fixed upon another policy. In January 1681 the king secured a pension from Louis, and used his new financial security to turn on the exclusionists. Ministers who had advocated the bill were sacked, and in March parliament was dissolved, never to be recalled in Charles's lifetime. Although William tried to patch up relations in a visit in July 1681, his trip was an ill-tempered affair. Charles was incensed by William's continuing demands that he negotiate with his legislature; James had become convinced that his nephew had been plotting with the whigs; and the new set of anti-exclusionist (or tory) ministers spread dark rumours about William's intentions. From 1681 the prince's relations with his uncles were set in a familiar—but now deeper and more dangerous—rut. Charles and James were so disappointed at William's refusal to be controlled that they suspected him of conspiring with their enemies. He had become so exasperated by Charles's refusal to work with parliament that he had shown himself willing to consider radical political solutions. From 1681 he was in contact with leaders of the whig party, for example meeting Arthur Capel, earl of Essex, and William, Lord Russell, during his trip to England that year.

For the rest of Charles's lifetime the new antagonism was chiefly revealed in the English king's anger that William offered refuge to his bitterest enemies. After the discovery of the 1683 Rye House plot to assassinate Charles some of the extreme whigs behind the conspiracy fled to the United Provinces, where they were allowed to live unmolested. Most outrageously for the king, the duke of Monmouth, who had been implicated in the plot, was received by William and entertained as a full member of the family. He went hunting with the prince over the summer of 1684, lived 'in great splendour' in one of his houses (Luttrell, *Brief Historical Relation*, 1.318), and was taken to plays, balls, and skating parties by Mary the following winter. Despite William's belief that Charles's anathemas against Monmouth were only for public consumption (and therefore that treating his son well accorded with the king's real, but secret, feelings), the hospitality did severe damage. The prince wrote submissive letters to the English court, but by the time Charles died in February 1685 the personal rupture was complete.

William and James II, 1685–1688

On James's accession there was a brief attempt by both the new monarch and the prince to improve relations. Cordial letters were exchanged, Monmouth was expelled from the United Provinces, and James refused to believe that his nephew had had anything to do with that duke's subsequent invasion of the west country in the early summer of 1685. This dawn, however, was false. As James began his controversial and prerogative-stretching campaign to emancipate his co-religionists old exasperations resurfaced. In England James's actions were condemned as attacks on his subjects' liberties and as a manifestation of Antichristian popery. The majority of Englishmen opposed the bullying of parliament to repeal anti-Catholic laws and the use of supposed royal powers to suspend these statutes. At William's court it is doubtful whether much sleep was lost over the rights of the Westminster parliament, or that the prince shared in hysterical anti-Catholicism, but James's policies were still deplored. William, in close contact with correspondents who suggested that opposition to the king was becoming desperate, feared that his uncle would plunge his realm into an internal conflict. If that happened, the stadholder knew, it would be impossible for England to be an effective counterweight to France. He would thus have lost his best chance of swinging the balance of European politics away from Louis. Accordingly William began to work to stop his uncle, either by persuasion, or by more conspiratorial methods.

For the first couple of years of James's reign William made few active interventions in British politics, preferring to collect information and gauge public opinion. In January 1687, however, the pace quickened when the prince sent Everard van Dijkvelt on a mission to London. The envoy was to inform the king that William wanted to support his uncle, but that support was conditional upon his abandoning attempts to change anti-Catholic laws without parliamentary consent. Dijkvelt was also permitted to make contact with opponents of the king. When James refused the Dutchman an early audience the mission began to look more like an attempt to build a Williamite party in England. Gilbert Burnet reported that Dijkvelt made contact with an assorted group of anti-court politicians and assured them that William backed their efforts against the king's policy. This group ranged across the spectrum from solid whigs such as Admiral Edward Russell, Henry Sidney, and William Cavendish, earl of Devonshire, through moderate figures such as George Savile, marquess of Halifax, and on to tories such as Danby and Bishop Henry Compton of London. It continued to meet with, and eventually to plot with, the prince's agents for the next eighteen months.

Over the summer of 1687 the Williamite opposition solidified further. Leading Englishmen travelled to The Hague
to consult with the prince, and in July William van Nassau
van Zuylestein, son of William's former governor, was
sent to London, officially to commiserate on the death of
James's mother-in-law, but unofficially to renew contacts
with British politicians and to set up a clandestine network of Williamite correspondents. The end of 1687 and
beginning of 1688 saw the writing and publication of *Pensionary Fagel's Letter: a Letter Writ by Mijn Heer Fagel
to Mr. James Stewart* (dated 4 November 1687 and published in 1688). This widely distributed and hugely successful pamphlet made William's religious stance clear. The
work stated that the stadholder opposed persecution, but it
also rejected unparliamentary suppression of anti-Catholic
statute, and implied that Britons should look to the prince
to stop James attacking their liberties. By the start of 1688,
therefore, William was locked in a dangerous dispute with
his uncle. Desperate to get James to reverse his policies, he
had launched a popularity contest with James in the king's
own realm.

Revolution, 1688–1689

The decision to invade

Over the winter of 1688–9 William invaded Britain and seized the Stuart crown. Debate about when he determined to do this has been vigorous, but since there is no direct evidence for the precise date of the decision the dispute will probably never be resolved. It is certain that William had wanted control of British foreign policy since at least 1672. It is equally clear, however, that, at least until the few months before the actual invasion, forcible seizure of the crown was not the most obvious way to secure this control. For example, it long seemed sensible for William to try to use his family connections to attract his uncles into alliance against France, or to support an anti-French party in the Stuart realm hoping it would become strong enough to force the court's hand. Again, the prince could simply have waited. Since Charles had had no legitimate children, and since it seemed unlikely that James would produce a son to displace Mary, William knew he should eventually come to control Britain as husband of its reigning queen. Given this, a date for his decision to invade as late as the spring 1688, and a date for his final resolution to be king as late as early December, look the most probable. He would not have risked uncertain invasions or usurpations until other possibilities had been exhausted.

Certainly military intervention had not been an attractive answer to William's difficulties in 1687. Although personal contact with James had broken down by the end of 1686, and although some of the hotter heads among the opposition to the king were already asking the prince to invade, William was building a party in Britain which might prove strong enough to stop the king, and he could still hope that Mary might soon inherit the crown. Over the winter of 1687–8, however, the situation began to change. On 10 December James announced officially that his wife was pregnant. Although this was not an instant disaster for the Orange party—the queen was ageing and had suffered miscarriages in the past—as time went by it looked increasingly possible that she would give birth to a live child, and if that child were a son, it would displace Mary from the succession. Over the same period it looked ever less probable that parliamentary opposition would halt James's career. The king stuck by his 1687 declaration of indulgence, which had used the prerogative to emancipate Catholics, and he continued a campaign to alter parliamentary franchises to secure a pliant legislature. William's contacts in England were full of despair, warning that the monarch's disregard of public opinion might soon result in civil war. By spring 1688, therefore, moderate methods of securing Britain for a united anti-French policy were looking hopeless, and the prince was starting to realize he would have to intervene to prevent the situation from running beyond his control.

Circumstances on the continent also increased the attractiveness of the military option. As 1688 wore on, it became increasingly likely that William could build an anti-French alliance of powers which could contain Louis while the prince crossed the channel. Spain had always looked to William to help it save its part of the Netherlands from France; the princes of western Germany had become increasingly worried by French expansion; and, crucially, on 9 May 1688 NS Frederick William of Brandenburg died. This last event elevated Frederick III to the electorate. The new ruler was more consistently opposed to Louis than his predecessor and, importantly, had hopes of being named William's heir. In the United Provinces, too, things began moving the prince's way. Conciliation after the disasters of 1684 built trust between the prince of Orange and Dutch political élites, and a series of near-suicidal decisions by the French to end the toleration of their protestant population (1685) and to impose punitive tariffs on Dutch goods (1687–8) alienated opinion in the Netherlands. By late spring even the Amsterdam-influenced states general was convinced there was no alternative to William's attempts to curb Louis.

Given this combination of circumstances it seems very likely that Gilbert Burnet was right to claim that the decision to invade was made about the beginning of May 1688. Even if a date as late as this is correct, however, it is still important to distinguish between a resolution to invade and one to seize the throne. Evidence about exactly when William decided to become king is once more very sketchy, but again it is unlikely that he made any firm resolve early, and it even seems probable that he delayed any final choice until well after the invasion was under way. The prince's main objective was to bring a united Stuart realm into the war with Louis. After spring 1688 invasion looked as if it might help this aim, as it could force James to accept a free parliament, which, given the political mood of the electorate, was likely to be fiercely anti-French. Going further and seizing the throne, by contrast, did not initially look as if it would unite the British against Versailles. Usurpation would be more controversial and difficult than simply forcing James to change his foreign policy, and it might leave the prince as a resented ruler, a position he knew from Dutch politics could rob him of influence. Given this analysis William was unlikely to have shut off options short of the throne until he had had a chance to see how well his military action went and how popular he was once he had arrived in England.

Preparations and appeals

Whatever was going on in William's mind in 1688, its consequences in outward actions were clear. From late spring the prince made multifaceted preparations to invade England. On the military side he began assembling a fleet at Hellevoetsluis. By autumn this was large enough to transport 21,000 troops, together with their horses, weapons and supplies. Politically, he squared the states general. Over the summer he convinced even a reluctant Amsterdam that a military build-up was necessary to contain an increasingly hostile France, and then revealed his complete plans, first to a secret session of the states of Holland on 29 September NS, and then to the states general on 8 October NS. On the diplomatic front he tried to calm the other powers of Europe, sending missions to Madrid, Vienna, and Brussels,

and himself travelling to Minden to speak to the new elector
of Brandenburg in September.

While this was going on in Europe, William's allies in the
Stuart realm were not neglected. By May the chief members
of his network of informers and correspondents had been
told he intended to invade and began to make preparations.
Their activities included consultations with Zuylestein, who
was sent to England in June (ostensibly to congratulate
James, who had, as feared, had a son); plans by the earls
of Danby and Devonshire to raise rebellions in the north
when William arrived; and attempts by Henry Sidney to
contact officers in James's army and persuade them to defect
to the prince when the invasion came. Most importantly, on
30 June the conspirators also issued an invitation to William
to intervene. This secret letter, signed by the 'immortal'
seven leaders of the plot, allowed the prince to claim that
he had gone to England because he had been asked to do so
by its citizens, and also reassured him of the success of the
enterprise by declaring that 'nineteen parts out of twenty
of the people throughout the kingdom' would support it
(Dalrymple, vol. 2, appendix, part 1, 228).

Perhaps as important as these military, diplomatic, and conspiratorial moves were William's ideological preparations.
The prince knew that invading another country would be
controversial: to avoid alienating his new European allies,
and to minimize resistance from the English population,
he would have to work hard to convince the world of the
justice of his actions. At the heart of this propaganda drive
was his manifesto, his *Declaration of Reasons for Appearing
in Arms in England*. Carefully drafted by Gaspar Fagel, this

offered an explanation for the invasion couched so as to avoid offence to its various audiences. Crucially, the manifesto took its stand on English law rather than religion. Claiming that William was intervening to stop James exceeding his prerogative, the prince prevented his action's resembling an anti-popish crusade, and so calmed the anxieties of Catholic states such as Spain and Austria. Equally crucially, the *Declaration* pitched for support from both whigs and tories. While it pleased the former group with its suggestion that monarchs should be held to account for illegal actions, it placated tories by concentrating on royal attacks upon their beloved Church of England, and by refusing to question James's right to the throne. The document placed the blame for recent policies on 'evil councillors' rather than the king himself, and eased fears that William had come to take the crown by stating he had 'nothing before his eyes' but a 'free and lawful parliament'. Once this brilliantly crafted pamphlet had been finished Fagel's propaganda machine distributed it with even more than its usual efficiency. It was translated into several languages, dispatched to foreign courts, and smuggled across the channel in thousands to be released as soon as William arrived in England.

Orange ambition

With all the preparations in place William was ready to move as soon as the wind would assist him over to England. For weeks it refused, and then storms dashed a first attempt at invasion launched on 29 October NS. After these early difficulties, however, William met with a success so complete that his propagandists could claim it was providential. Sailing out on 11 November NS he made stately progress down the channel on a north-easterly which kept the English fleet bottled up in the mouth of the Thames, and then took advantage of a sudden change of wind direction to bring him into the convenient harbour of Torbay.

After landing unopposed on 15 November NS—5 November OS, so an auspicious anniversary for protestant deliverance— William made his way rapidly to Exeter, where he set up a command centre and a printing press. For the first few days there was some concern at the lack of overt support from the local population. While crowds had cheered his early progress, and almost no forcible opposition had been shown, few Englishmen had rallied to the prince's banner. Over the next weeks, however, these worries largely vanished as local gentry started to muster at Exeter; as news arrived from the north of risings in favour of William under Danby; and as a series of pre-planned defections started from James's army officers. William could therefore march east from Exeter on 21 November with some confidence. By this time James's position had virtually collapsed. He had joined his forces on Salisbury Plain on 19 November, but was so badly shaken by rebellions, defections, and his own uncontrollable nose-bleeds that he took the advice of his army council to avoid immediate battle and retreated to London on the 23rd.

Once back in the capital the king bought time by sending commissioners to treat with William at Hungerford, but bundled his wife and son out of the country and then attempted to join them on 10 December. When news of the king's flight led to riotous panic in the capital (rumours circulated that James had gone to lead an attack by a wild Irish force on the city) William's triumph was complete.

The corporation of London invited him into the capital to maintain order on 11 December and he arrived to heed their call on the 18th, somewhat farcically slipping into Westminster through St James's Park and thus missing the huge crowds that had gathered to welcome him along the Oxford road.

Up to this point William's success had exceeded all expectations. Now, however, and repeating the pattern of earlier parts of his career, the prince's very success began to work against him. The problem stemmed primarily from an inflation of the prince's ambition. Now that he had seen evidence of popular support, and now that James was broken, he definitely decided to take the throne. Whereas his statements and actions before James's flight suggested he was still keeping his options open—even at the Hungerford negotiations he had offered terms which gave James hope of keeping his crown—after mid-December it was clear he wished to cut off any solution but his own accession. When, for example, James was captured on 13 December in Faversham and taken back to London, William did his best to get him out of the way. The prince insisted his uncle stay first at Ham—ostensibly 'for the greater safety of his person' (Japikse, 1.1.25–6), but actually because he would be too far from London to whip up support—and then that he be allowed to go to Rochester, whence everybody knew he would renew his flight to France. Similarly, when William arrived in the capital he made himself its effective master. He benefited from his wife's agreement to stay behind in Holland (as she was the closest relative of James not under his control, many English people thought she herself might have a claim to the throne); he garrisoned London with his own élite Dutch troops; and he ordered Danby and his forces to stay in the north where they would have less influence. Even by itself such presumption might have cost support. What made it even more damaging was that William had promised in his manifesto that his sole aim was a free parliament. The obvious mismatch between the prince's behaviour and his propaganda allowed James's supporters to accuse William of hypocrisy, while people such as Sir Edward Seymour who had joined the prince 'on the bottom of his *Declaration*' began to fear they had been duped (*Correspondence of…Clarendon*, 2.238). William thus faced a situation in which he now wanted the throne but found his path to it hindered by piles of his own pamphlets.

William's response to this problem was partly to shift the focus of his propaganda. It is noticeable that from mid-December his spokesmen placed far more emphasis on his role as a providential deliverer than on legal arguments. Providentialism contained a strong case for William's elevation, but had not been compromised by earlier statements about the English constitution. Perhaps as importantly, William devised a strategy which he hoped would secure him the throne, while appearing to stay true to his original position. He continued to insist that the English legislature must be free to decide on a settlement of English government, but simultaneously moved to deny it any real alternative to offering him the crown. The first element of this strategy was initiated in two meetings late in December. The earlier of these, on 21 December, was with all peers present in London; the later, on 26 December, was with MPs who survived from Charles II's days. These irregular, but arguably parliamentary, bodies heard the prince repeat his commitment to 'the end of [his] *Declaration*', and then agreed to help him secure the free legislature which that document had demanded (Cobbett, *Parliamentary History*, 5, 21, 23 Dec 1688). They summoned a convention which was to be constituted as if it were a parliament, and which would be at liberty to decide the succession. Upholding the appearance of free parliamentary choice, William did little to influence the elections to the convention held in January and then said nothing publicly about his ambitions, either in his letter to the convention on its meeting on 22 January or when it immediately fell into bitter debates about whether to offer the crown to the prince, to declare him regent for James, or to award the throne to Mary.

While the formal freedom of the English to decide their future was preserved, however, the other part of William's strategy was also in place. Continuing to garrison the southeast of England with Dutch troops, he made himself the only guarantor of order at a time when many feared prolonged constitutional crisis would return the country to civil war. He thus achieved a position of overwhelming influence, since a threat on his part to withdraw if he did not get the throne would be absolutely terrifying. As division in the convention delayed any settlement through the first week of February, William played this trump card, letting convention members know that he would return to Holland if he were not offered the crown. Realizing that the choice now was between William or anarchy, opponents of the prince's elevation gave way. He was offered the crown, and finally felt safe to invite Mary to join him in England.

In a ceremony in the Guildhall on 13 February 1689 William was given the throne on four conditions which—while they did something to remodel the English monarchy—were acceptable to William because they would not hamper his ability to mobilize England against France. First, William had to share the throne with his wife in a novel 'joint monarchy'. Mary was formally included to minimize the appearance of a break in the succession, but this did not limit the king since the settlement bestowed the actual executive power of the crown on William alone. Secondly, the new king had to accept new oaths of loyalty which implied that he was only a *de facto* rather than *de jure* monarch. This was done by removing the words 'rightful and lawful' from the clause describing William's title, but while this might seem to weaken the king's claims, it actually helped him by allowing reluctant tories to proclaim obedience. Thirdly, William could not accept the throne before he had listened to a 'declaration of rights' outlining the limits of royal pre-rogatives. This gave definition to traditional—but vague— bans on unparliamentary armies, taxes, and suspension of laws, but was less radical than it might have been since William had used his influence to kill any wholesale reduc-tion in the monarchy's powers, and evaded any explicit recognition that the declaration's terms were conditions of his taking the throne (*Declaration of the Lords Spiritual*). Fourthly, William had to acknowledge the right of his sister-in-law Anne, and her children, to succeed before any off-spring he had by a wife after Mary. This condition was imposed to calm fears about the importation of a wholly foreign dynasty, but would not, of course, affect the king's own terms of rule.

Overall, therefore, William had gained almost the whole authority of a Stuart king, less than fifteen weeks after landing at Torbay. The rapidly arranged coronation, held on 11 April, did a little more to curtail the monarch's power with its new oath binding the ruler to 'the Statutes in Parliament agreed on' (*An Account of the Ceremonial*). In essence, however, the ceremony confirmed that William had most of the old prerogative, including control over armies, foreign policy, the appointment of ministers, and the supreme governorship of the church. Supporters of William thought this success so remarkable that the 'Finger of God was visibly in it' (Tillotson, 26), and the word 'glorious' was officially attached to the revolution as early as 22 January 1689 (*An Order of the Lords*). Cynics, by contrast, might note a remarkable similarity with 1672. Once again the prince had publicly denied any wish to be raised to head of a nation, but had claimed to have bowed to the will of the people, the call of their representatives, and the manifest intentions of heaven. Once again, however, force, propaganda, and careful manipulation of mob violence had played a greater part than William might wish to admit.

The struggle with France, 1689–1702

Securing the thrones: the French and Jacobite challenge

Given the extraordinary nature of his accession, William had surprisingly little difficulty making himself secure on the throne of England and Wales. Although not all the political nation welcomed his elevation, few thought there was any real alternative in February 1689, and most continued to accept the new king, either to keep out the papist James or because supporting the *de facto* regime brought more stability than working for a Stuart restoration. It is true that William had difficulties with the old king's officer corps in the army. Only a third of these agreed to serve the new regime, and there was a series of mutinies over spring and summer 1689. It is also true that more than 300 'nonjuring' clergy, including seven bishops, refused to swear the oaths to the new monarchs; that some leading English politicians made contact with James II in the early 1690s; and that Louis XIV offered sporadic succour to the exiled king and to his 'Jacobite' supporters. As a result a Jacobite underground survived throughout William's reign: groups of conspirators published subversive literature, planned rebellions (there were major plots in 1690, 1692, 1694, and 1696), and tried to persuade the French to invade to help the cause. Yet despite all this, William's rule was never in serious danger in England. As we shall see, his wife was loyal and helped to focus pro-Stuart sentiment towards the new regime, while overt support for her father was limited. Early difficulties with the army were overcome; nonjurors were deprived and then proved politically quietist; most of those who made contact with James did it only as a political insurance policy; and all Jacobite plots were uncovered before they became dangerous.

In Ireland, by contrast, William faced three years of hard struggle to gain control. Legally his task should have been easy. The Irish crown was joined to that of England, so technically William and Mary acceded in Dublin when accepting the crown in London. In reality, however, Ireland was always going to be difficult to procure. Its majority Catholic population had done well under James II and rapidly came to support the declaration of loyalty to the old king made by the lord lieutenant, Richard Talbot, earl of Tyrconnell. By spring 1689 only isolated towns in protestant Ulster were in William's hands and, worse, the French had sent troops to aid James as he set up government in Dublin. William thus had to take urgent action, both to make good his claim to Ireland and to ensure the country did not become a dangerous base from which Jacobites and Louis might attack Britain.

At first William was frustrated in his campaign to recapture his westernmost realm. Although he repeatedly stressed 'the dangers grown too great' in Ireland in his speeches to the Westminster parliament (*Journals of the House of Lords*, 14, 1685–1691, 128), he himself was unable to lead a force in 1689 since he needed to settle affairs in London, and the army he sent to Ulster became bogged down by poor weather and a supply system so corrupt as to become the subject of a major Commons investigation. Over the early months of 1690 things improved somewhat as the king freed additional soldiers for the Irish theatre, dismissed English ministers who had opposed his leading an expedition there, and sailed to Ireland—he landed at Carrickfergus on 14 June. His arrival, with enthusiastic preachers and with 15,000 extra troops (Danish and Dutch as well as English), lifted morale and by 1 July he was facing James II across the River Boyne outside Dublin.

In some ways the ensuing battle was the greatest success of William's career. When the bulk of James's forces, believing that an enemy flanking manoeuvre was going to be the main attack, marched west from the main point of confrontation, William himself led a charge through the water and threatened to trap the Jacobites in a bend of the stream before they retreated in some disorder. However, while this victory led both to James's withdrawal from Dublin and to the steady evacuation of French troops, it was not as complete a salvation as its subsequent celebration by Irish protestants would suggest. The Jacobites avoided rout on the battlefield and then proved strong enough to trouble William for another fifteen months. Although the English king occupied Dublin on 2 July and then marched west, he still suffered severe military setbacks, such as the capture of his artillery at Ballyneety on 12 August and his failure to take Limerick later that month. Thus when William returned to Britain in September, he may have ended any possibility that his other kingdoms might be invaded from Dublin, but he had been diverted from the struggle against Louis on the European mainland and had not quelled resistance in Munster and Connaught. Williamite commanders such as Godard van Ginkel would have to campaign for much of 1691, and offer extraordinarily generous terms for surrender, before they achieved that objective.

Securing Scotland was less difficult than gaining Ireland but was rather more complicated than the revolution in England. Things began smoothly enough for William. In December 1688 he met waves of Scots magnates who had streamed south realizing that he was now the effective power on the island. At a gathering of almost the entire Scottish political nation in London on 7 January William accepted responsibility for maintaining order north of the border, and sent out letters ordering the Scottish estates to convene. This body met as a constitutional convention on 14 March 1689 and immediately set about resolving who should be king of Scotland. For a moment it was not clear that William would carry the day as many members still leaned towards James, but soon the new English monarch's tact in dealing with parliamentary bodies won through. When letters from William and his rival were read out to the convention on the 16th, members were flattered by William's assurance that 'it lyes to you to enter upon such consultations as are most probably to settle you' (*Acts of the Parliaments of Scotland, 1689–1702*, 9), but were alienated by James's 'Threats and Promises' (*An Account of the Proceedings*). Once the leading Jacobite, John Graham of Claverhouse, had stormed out of the convention the way was clear for it to declare that James had 'forfaulted' the throne, and for William and Mary to accept a joint monarchy of Scotland (where William became William II) in a ceremony in London on 11 May.

After this good start, however, William's progress in the north faltered. First, the Scottish estates proved far more willing than the English parliament to press its rights and take advantage of the crisis of monarchy. In April 1689 the convention approved two documents—the 'claim of right' and the 'articles of grievance'—which asserted a vigorous interpretation of parliamentary power, declared crown-appointed episcopacy intolerable, and demanded the abolition of the 'Lords of the Articles' (the committee of the estates dominated by royal ministers which approved the Scottish privy council's actions when the full parliament was not sitting). To William, these calls were outrageous. They cut away at the means by which he hoped to control Scotland, and he feared that radical calls for the abolition of bishops would worsen divisions in a nation riven between episcopalians and presbyterians. William did not, therefore, commit himself clearly to the claim or the articles when accepting the throne; he opposed the translation of their demands into parliamentary legislation throughout 1689; and briefly tried to distract Scots with suggestions for a parliamentary union with England. Yet while the king's displeasure was clear, his political weakness was also obvious. Over the summer and autumn the estates blocked any vote of supply and threatened to make the kingdom ungovernable. As a result William was forced into a humiliating retreat. Although he had prorogued the parliament in anger on 2 August 1689, when it met again in March 1690 he conceded its demands. The Lords of the Articles were abolished along with episcopacy and the royal supremacy over the church, so that the final revolution settlement in Scotland proved far more damaging to William's formal power than that in England.

A second development to trouble William in Scotland was a Jacobite rising. When Graham of Claverhouse left the convention in April 1689 he did not limit himself to this protest, but rode north to raise the highland clans for the old king's cause. On 27 July his victory at Killiecrankie seemed to open up the lowlands to his forces, and only his death on the battlefield (which left the resistance leaderless) saved the fledgeling Edinburgh regime. Fortunately for William the Jacobites were decisively defeated at Dunkeld on 21 August, and this ended any threat to southern Scotland. However, resistance in some highland areas smouldered on until 1692, and was only ended by granting indemnities to clans who would swear loyalty, along with the treacherous slaughter of the MacDonalds at Glencoe. In general, therefore, the pattern of events in Scotland reflected the broader picture of William's securing control in the British Isles. At the metropolitan core, political acceptance of the new regime was surprisingly rapid and complete. This still meant, however, that extensive military action and political compromise were necessary to counter opposition elsewhere.

The war in Europe, 1689–1697

William had invaded the Stuart realms in order to bring their resources into conflict with Louis XIV. While he had been preparing and executing his expedition, the need to do this had become even more pressing as the French king had resumed his eastward expansion. Ignoring William's threat to England, Louis had decided to try to cow the German princes by invading the Rhineland in the autumn of 1688, and had then declared war on the United Provinces once the recently emboldened Netherlands refused to acquiesce in his actions. Thus containment of France would have to remain William's priority, and it is therefore essential to describe his continuing military and diplomatic action against Versailles before examining his longer-term relations with his new subjects. In almost every area of domestic policy the king's decisions were shaped by the progress of his struggle, and the need to maintain support for it.

The first stage in William's new attempt to stop French expansion was completed over the first half of 1689 as he mobilized most of Europe against his old enemy. His earliest success was with the United Provinces. Reassured that Britain would not be thrown into the scales against them, the states general held firm in the face of Louis's declaration of war. In fact, William had very little difficulty mobilizing the Netherlands in the years after 1689. The old peace party was disabled by Louis's intransigence; and although Fagel had died in 1688, robbing William of one of his ablest political allies in the provinces, the stadholder found a brilliant new pensionary in Anthonie Heinsius. This new agent managed Dutch politics successfully during William's long absences, consulting the Amsterdam regents sufficiently to keep them on board, and outmanoeuvring republican party factions in that city in the early 1690s. When Heinsius's skill was added to continued outpourings of Orange propaganda, and to the fact that the prince was no longer present to irritate the regents with his hauteur (he spent the bulk of his time after 1689 in England or at the battlefront in Flanders), William's dominance of Dutch politics was secure.

Coronation in England, meanwhile, gave William a chance to press his new realm into the battle with Louis. Benefiting from horror that the French supported the Jacobite rising in Ireland, William persuaded the Westminster parliament to participate in the fight. On 5 May England declared war, and she was in turn joined by the other members of a 'grand alliance' (Scotland, Austria, Spain, Savoy, and many German states) which the stadholder-king negotiated over the next two months. This alliance determined to reduce France to her 1659 borders and agreed to block any future Bourbon claims to the throne of Spain by promoting the Austrian Habsburgs as rightful heirs to the Spanish empire when its ruler, Carlos II, died.

After this early diplomatic success, however, things went badly. William was kept away from the European battle-field by English politics in 1689 and by the campaign in Ireland the next year, and during his absence the French defeated the English navy at Beachy Head in June 1690, and captured Fleurus in July. In 1691 William crossed back to the Netherlands for the first time since 1688. He received a triumphal welcome in The Hague that demonstrated a strong hold on Dutch public opinion, but his presence on the continent did not prevent the French taking Mons, and still worse catastrophes followed during his visits to Flanders over the next two years. In June 1692 the French captured Namur, despite the fact that 40,000 English troops were in Flanders with their king, and William's attempt to storm the

French camp at Steenkerke on 3 August NS ended in disaster. In July 1693 the French army defeated William and inflicted 16,000 casualties at Landen, while in October they went on to capture Charleroi.

The next two years saw a brief respite in the string of defeats, and—as we shall see—the king developed a good working relationship with his wife, allowing her to manage domestic affairs during the summers when he fought in the Low Countries. In 1694 William captured Huy, thus reversing most of Louis's gains of 1693, and on 5 September 1695 NS he managed to recapture Namur. However, by this stage war strains in England and the Netherlands were starting to show. Both countries endured heavy taxation and disruption to trade routes; Holland was experiencing an economic depression which led to rioting in Amsterdam in February 1696; and England was suffering a crisis of public credit and a collapse in confidence in a coinage devalued by clipping and the shipment of specie to Flanders. When these difficulties caused an effective cessation of payments to the army over the summer of 1696 it was clear the allied war effort could not continue much longer. As early as 1692 William had realized that his stated aim of reversing all of France's recent gains was impractical, and he had consequently begun four years of secret contacts with Louis to explore terms for a possible peace. In 1696 these feelers were taken seriously by a French king whose country was equally exhausted, and in May real bargaining started between Dijkvelt and François de Callières—though English and Dutch politicians were still not informed. The principle of a return to the territorial position of 1688 was quickly agreed but discussions dragged for months over whether and at what point Louis would have formally to accept William as king of the Stuart realms. As a result open diplomatic negotiations did not start until May 1697, and the treaty of Ryswick was not signed until September. Under this all territories captured by any side since 1688 were handed back; the Dutch were allowed to garrison eight 'barrier' fortresses in the Spanish Netherlands; Louis promised not to aid William's enemies and finally recognized him as rightful king in London; and the town of Orange was handed back to its ruling prince.

Diplomacy and its failure, 1697–1702

Although some of the terms of the Ryswick peace were useful to William, it is hard not to regard the settlement as a disappointment for him on a scale comparable to 1678. He had been forced to stop fighting before France was definitely defeated; Louis had kept most of his recent gains; French recognition of William was rapidly called into question as it became clear James would not be ejected from his lodgings near Paris; and, most frustratingly, the issue of the Spanish succession was left out of the treaty, keeping open the possibility that the Bourbons would gain a massive prize on Carlos II's death. As if to underline William's failure, his plans to keep up a large English army to threaten and contain Louis were thwarted by a war-weary Westminster parliament in the two years after the peace. Arguing that a standing army was a drain on national resources and a threat to English liberties, MPs used their powers to cut the forces to 7000 men by the end of 1699—far too small a figure to impress foreign powers.

As a result of these reversals William entered the post-Ryswick world greatly weakened. Therefore, when he was faced with the problem of what to do about Spain he resorted to diplomacy, rather than military threat, to try to contain the French. Relying on Louis's own reluctance to go back to war after a long bruising conflict, William used Heinsius and his new confidant, Arnold Joost van Keppel, to approach Versailles with offers to divide the Spanish empire. Without consulting his wartime allies, or the domestic governments of either Britain or the Netherlands, William negotiated the first partition treaty (1 October 1698). This proposed to grant Spain, the Indies, and the Spanish Netherlands to Joseph Ferdinand, the electoral prince of Bavaria, while compensating the French with Naples and Tuscany and the Austrians with Milan. When this deal was undone four months later by the death of the electoral prince, William renegotiated, again consulting no-one outside his immediate circle. The second partition treaty (15 March 1700) granted to the Bourbons Spain's Italian possessions and gave the rest of her empire to the Austrian emperor's second son on the understanding that the main branch of the Habsburg family would never inherit them.

At first sight the partition treaties seemed to offer a chance for a new beginning in relations between Louis and William. Twice in two years the old enemies had concluded agreements which would have allowed the English king to contain his French counterpart without further European warfare. Unfortunately, however, circumstances soon swept the two men back towards conflict. Partition was popular nowhere outside the monarchs' courts, and the principle was soon effectively dead. While English and Dutch politicians were angry that they had been kept in the dark during the negotiations and were worried that the French had been granted too much power in the Mediterranean, partition was effectively scuppered by the refusal of either the Spanish or Austrian governments to accept it. Consequently, when Carlos finally died in October 1700, leaving his entire inheritance to Louis's second grandson, Philip of Anjou, the French monarch accepted the will. With Spain and Austria against partition, Versailles realized that imposing the superseded treaty would bring war as certainly as betraying William, and braced itself against the stadholder-king's anger.

William's initial response to French actions was to try to rescue partition. In spring 1701 he offered terms to Louis, under which Philip could keep Spain and the Indies, if the Austrians could be compensated with old Spanish territories in Italy. In April he even recognized Philip as king of Spain. Yet in the end Louis's intransigence killed this compromise, and William was forced to try to remobilize the grand alliance. At first this was difficult. Although Austria was willing to fight for her claims on the Spanish empire, and the Dutch remained solid behind their captain-general, others were less committed. Many Spaniards were happy to accept Philip as monarch; the German princes were still wary of war; and much of the English parliament thought the accession of a separate, cadet, branch of the Bourbons to the whole Spanish empire was better than granting its Italian possessions to the main branch as partition had done.

However, despite this inauspicious start, actions by Louis over 1701 steadily consolidated his old foes behind William.

In February French troops occupied the Dutch barrier fortresses in the Spanish Netherlands and in September, on the death of James II, Louis reversed the position he had taken at Ryswick and recognized the exiled monarch's son as rightful king of England. Consequently William was able to pull the old alliance slowly back towards war. In April 1701 the English Commons voted to support the Dutch in the face of French threat, and on 12 June the same body voted to restore the old wartime alliances with Austria and the United Provinces. In The Hague on 7 September NS William formally achieved this restoration with the second grand alliance. Under this the British kingdoms, the Netherlands, and the empire agreed to seek a Habsburg succession to Spain. They also agreed to seek further allies to pursue these goals, and that war would have to ensue if they could not be secured by diplomacy. Thus by the time William died in March 1702 he had placed Europe back on the road to military action against France.

Monarch and politician, 1689–1702

Politics at Westminster

As William tried to contain Louis in Europe he faced quite as difficult a challenge in maintaining English support for that containment. Unless he could preserve his new realm's early willingness to counter French ambitions, his entire continental strategy would be in danger. English resources were vital to his military efforts: England's armed preparedness was essential to maintain any credible diplomatic pressure on Versailles.

Unfortunately, maintaining England's commitment was not easy. Most demandingly, William was faced with persuading the Westminster parliament to back his policies. Not only had the events of 1688–9 boosted legislators' confidence about their place in the polity, it was obvious that the new king could not rule without parliament, since it would have to consent to the taxes needed to finance his war. Moreover, political circumstances made it difficult to unite parliamentarians behind an aggressive foreign policy in the 1690s. At a basic level, William's origins raised suspicions that the king had Dutch rather than English interests at heart. Throughout the reign parliamentary speeches voiced concern that England had been tricked into conflict which could not benefit her, but merely served Holland's security. Moreover, William's war stoked renewed legislative fears of court corruption and arbitrary power. Because conflict gave the king huge revenues and vast armies, many feared English liberty would be lost to military coercion or political bribery, and some referred back to William's early behaviour in the United Provinces to suggest that he might try to rule unchecked. Finally, party battles threatened any united support for the king's policies. Bitter rivalry between whigs and tories survived 1689; as a result factional enemies could be relied upon to stir up trouble for any statesmen co-operating with William.

The king's response to these difficulties can be described in terms of three main strategies. First, to convince the English that containing Louis was essential, he embarked on a wide-ranging propaganda campaign. Centring on royal speeches to parliament, sermons, pamphlets, and a series of fasts and thanksgivings, this sought to convince the English that opposing the French was both their protestant duty (since Louis was an antichristian persecutor), and in their prudential interest (since the French king was also potential 'universal monarch', ambitious to destroy the autonomy of all other nations). Secondly, to reduce parliamentary suspicion of the court, William attempted to win confidence by defusing points of tension between the executive and the legislature. Although he was occasionally outraged that parliament 'used him like a dog' (Foxcroft, 2.207), and although he had a personal preference for retaining the old prerogatives of the crown, William had learned in the Netherlands that co-operation with powerful representative assemblies was the only viable policy. He thus allowed parliament to examine areas of executive expenditure and action which it had never scrutinized before, and he retreated—at least ultimately—in the face of its campaigns to limit his powers. Finally, to deal with party battles the king made it clear he would never become a prisoner of one faction. He refused to countenance witch-hunts by one grouping against the other (especially discouraging retrospective investigations into politicians' actions before 1689), and he made it clear that the way was always open for oppositions to come back into office if they could offer more effective leadership of the war and parliament.

Crown in parliament

On accepting the crown William's task was to assemble an administration which could organize the conflict with Louis. At first he attempted to ease political tensions by sharing political prizes. He balanced one whig secretary of state, Charles Talbot, twelfth earl of Shrewsbury, with a tory, Daniel Finch, earl of Nottingham, and, while he appointed many hot whigs to the administration, he also rewarded his old tory friend Danby with the lord presidency. Unfortunately, however, partisan rivalries rapidly destroyed this even-handed strategy, and soon had the king expressing outrage at ministers' attempts to undermine their colleagues. Although tories upset him by demanding a generous revenue for his sister-in-law Anne (who had set up a rival court to his own), whigs infuriated him even more with a series of attempts to prosecute tories for their actions under the king's two predecessors. As William pressed an indemnity for past crimes to cool the political temperature, whigs demanded investigations of these transgressions—so that by July 1689 the king had convinced himself that they were stirring up trouble in hopes of bringing in a republic.

In these circumstances William began to abandon his earlier ties with the whigs, and confided ever more closely with the tory earl of Nottingham. By the start of 1690, when the whigs finally alienated the king by opposing his plans to join the war in Ireland, the alliance between the two men was complete. To the bitter denunciations of Nottingham's enemies (the whig comptroller of the household, Tom Wharton, went as far as to write to the king questioning his monarch's honesty), William swung behind the tories, and called a general election early in February 1690. Although breaking with earlier royal practice by refusing to use the court's influence to help his favoured politicians (the king was still determined to prove he was a monarch above party), the new parliament provided Nottingham with a working Commons majority, and the king made ministerial changes which removed many, though not all, whigs from office.

The main problem for the new ministry was parliamentary suspicion of the executive. This had been apparent as early as 1689; then, fears about royal power had led the Commons to delay its customary grant of the revenue from customs and excise to the king for life, and suspicions continued through the early 1690s as the war continued to go badly. While the king finally secured a revenue settlement in spring 1690, this granted only customs for life and insisted that excise revenue be reviewed again in four years time. Similarly the period to the mid-decade was dominated by attempts to scale back royal influence over parliament through 'place' legislation to evict government employees from the Commons and 'triennial' legislation to force the king to call a new general election every three years. William's reaction to these campaigns was hostile. Determined to preserve traditional royal influence over the legislature, he mobilized supporters in the two houses to defeat place and triennial bills in 1692, and then used the royal veto on a triennial measure in 1693 and a place bill early the next year. The last incident almost led to a constitutional crisis. An outraged Commons sent an address to the king on 27 January 1694, accusing him of listening to 'the secret advice' of evil counsellors and suggesting he had no right to use his veto. William only just managed to calm matters on the last day of the month by responding that he would 'ever have a great regard for the advice of parliaments'—an ambiguous phrase, but one accepted by at least a majority of the house as a promise not to reject bills again (Cobbett, *Parliamentary History*, 5, 31 January 1694).

Yet while William's attachment to the crown's old influence over parliament soured relations with that body, his strategy of co-operating with it wherever possible produced a more productive relationship in the field of public finance. As early as 28 June 1689—and pretty much unprompted—William offered the Commons scrutiny of the public accounts. He wanted, he said, to prove 'how very little of the Revenue has been applied to any other Use, than that of the Navy and the Land forces' (*Journals of the House of Commons*, 10, 1688–1689, 200). This was an extraordinary move, inviting parliament into an area which had long been

regarded as the monarch's private business. The next year
William went further, floating the idea of a parliamentary
commission of public accounts which would meet regularly
to audit the government's activities. Although this body produced some damning accounts of financial mismanagement
after it was established in 1691, it would be wrong to see
it as the core of a 'country' opposition. It formed part of
the king's strategy of working with parliament; it harnessed
Commons suspicion of the executive to the useful task of
rooting out waste and corruption in the management of the
war, and William consequently thanked the commissioners
for their work on even the most hostile reports. In the end,
conciliation also won through in other areas. William calmly
accepted the limitations of his 1690 revenue settlement; he
allowed a triennial bill to pass in 1694; he permitted a series
of parliamentary investigations into public servants between
1689 and 1696; and he co-operated with the establishment
of the 'civil list' which effectively granted the Commons
control of all finance except that sum needed to run the
king's household and civil administration. Overall the king
did enough to forestall any breakdown in relations between
court and parliament. Legislative support for the war was
remarkably solid. By 1695 parliament was voting over
£4 million a year in tax revenue, and had begun to construct
innovative systems of long-term funded government debt.

Party and pragmatism

However, if William's strategy of working with parliament
saved his war effort, it could not save Nottingham's administration. Despite his guiding the country through William's

early absences in Ireland and Flanders, the secretary of state was attacked mercilessly for presiding over the maladministrations uncovered by the Commons, and for the disastrous course of the war in the early 1690s. By 1693 his position was so weak that even the king began to realize the unpopularity of his trusted minister might damage support for the conflict. William consequently asked for Nottingham's resignation on 6 November, though he told him he was convinced of the earl's 'fidelity and zeal to his service' (Horwitz, 146). By this time the king was turning back towards a group of court or junto whigs led by Sir John Somers, who had tried to gain his favour by abandoning destructive factional posturing. Encouraged by the advice of Robert Spencer, second earl of Sunderland—a man who had been a close adviser to James and so himself benefited from William's determination not to damn people for their political pasts—the king began to see this group as a ministry which might control the Commons. Consequently he appointed Somers lord keeper early in 1693, and brought back many other whigs— along with Sunderland himself—following Nottingham's dismissal. By the end of 1695 even William's old ally Danby had been eased out, and in February 1696 a failed Jacobite assassination plot against William weakened the tories further. As always, the conspiracy was discovered before it presented any real threat to the king, but it did give the whigs an opportunity to benefit from a surge of support for the endangered monarch. An 'association' was drawn up in the Commons promising vengeance on William's enemies, but many tories found they could not sign it because it referred to the king as 'rightful and lawful', and would therefore force them beyond *de facto* loyalty (*Manuscript of House of Lords*, new ser., 2.204). Despite the king's discouragement of the association movement (he was still determined not to anathematize either party), whigs used the opportunity to denounce their rivals as crypto-Jacobites, and winkled them out of many national and local offices.

Yet while the whigs appeared to have triumphed, their position was no more secure than Nottingham's had been, given William's willingness to look to another party if his ministers failed to promote his containment of Louis XIV. Indeed, since the king's personal relations with the junto (except Somers) were cool, it is arguable that they were on even shakier ground. It was, therefore, no surprise when they were removed in 1699 after years of declining success in delivering the king's policies.

The whigs' central problem was that, like Nottingham, they could not dispel suspicion of the court's ambition in the House of Commons. This became particularly apparent in 1697, when the junto had to defend William's unpopular desire for a peacetime standing army. After the treaty of Ryswick the king was determined to contain Louis by retaining an effective English force of about 35,000 men. In his speech opening parliament on 3 December 1697 he stated that England could not be 'safe' without a substantial military capability (*Journals of the House of Lords*, 16, 1696–1701, 174). A 'new country' opposition, however, disagreed. Now led by Robert Harley, and bringing together tories and dissident whigs, it argued that a standing army would be an expensive threat to English liberties. Capitalizing on popular hostility to the military, Harley launched a series of parliamentary attacks on the junto, and succeeded in cutting troop numbers to just 10,000 by the end of the 1697–8 session.

The court's response to this assault was confused, and fatally soured relations between king and ministers. William, incensed that his judgement was being questioned in an area vital to his struggle with France, adopted an unusually intransigent attitude. He continued to demand large forces in speeches to parliament; he refused to allow the whigs to suggest 15,000 soldiers as a compromise figure in the debates of 1697–8; and over the summer of 1698 he attempted to defy parliament by hiding troops in the Irish establishment and among the officer corps. As a result the Commons reassembled in the autumn of 1698 in even more belligerent mood. On discovering that William had retained 14,834 men rather than 10,000, it voted to reduce numbers by another 3000, and so outraged the king still further. During the session William refused to allow his ministers to argue for 10,000, and started to talk of leaving England, perhaps permanently. On 29 December he told Somers he intended to leave England since the nation entertained such 'distrust and jealousies of him' (*Private and Original Correspondence of…Shrewsbury*, 572–3). Over the next month Somers was able to talk William back into his more usual policy of bowing to parliament, so that the king's speech on 1 February 1699 accepted army disbandment on the ground that rupture between monarch and legislature was even 'more fatal' than leaving the kingdom undefended (*Journals of the House of Lords*, 16, 1696–1701, 372). Unfortunately, however, the lord chancellor could not improve relations between monarch and junto. In 1698 the king had shown his disgust at the whigs' failure to save the army by refusing to support them in the general election of that year. In 1699 he calmly accepted the resignations of leading junto figures frightened of Commons impeachment if they stayed in office, and on 27 April 1700 dismissed even Somers after the minister had failed to stop parliament reconfiscating lands in Ireland which the king had granted to his supporters.

The loss of the whigs left William without a strong ministerial team. On past practice the king would have turned to the tories, but in 1699–1700 he delayed, angry at that party's role in disbanding his forces. Consequently junto ministers were replaced by stopgaps. Quite rapidly, however, the king's strategy of working with anyone who could work with him (whatever even their recent past) won through. Over the winter of 1699–1700 Robert Harley gained credit for piloting the king's supply through the Commons from the backbenches as the junto administration collapsed, and William was consequently converted to negotiations with tories. By December 1700 the king had concluded a deal under which Harley's allies Laurence Hyde, first earl of Rochester, and Sidney Godolphin would gain major posts in the administration; parliament would be dissolved to try to increase the number of supporters of the new ministry; and the king would support Harley's campaign for the speakership of the Commons when it reconvened. The fruits of this deal came in the spring of 1701. Harley was elected to the chair in February, and then piloted through the Act of Settlement, which finally blasted the hopes of the exiled Stuarts. The act stated that should both William and Anne die without heirs—now a virtual certainty, since the death of Anne's only surviving child, William, duke of Gloucester, in July 1700—the throne would pass to the Hanoverian electors.

Yet again, however, William's co-operation with his new ministry was no guarantee that he would not look back towards the alternative party as soon as trouble arose. As the French threat re-emerged in the last months of the king's life, the whigs positioned themselves as the people most enthusiastic to return to war, and so began to appeal to a monarch who found his own country-tory ministers still worried about the advantages which conflict handed to the court. Urging a vigorous response to Louis's occu-pation of the barrier fortresses, the junto looked more nat-ural allies of the king than an administration which coun-selled caution and denounced agitation outside parliament for a return to battle. Worse still, in April 1701 the tories offended William by attempting to impeach leading junto whigs for negotiating the partition treaties. This was not only grossly unfair—since the ministers had known almost nothing about the king's diplomacy—but also questioned the king's judgement in foreign policy. As a result William began to wonder if he was backing the correct party, and once again consulted Sunderland. The earl urged one last swing back to the whigs, and by October 1701 the king was negotiating with Somers. In November parliament was dissolved on request from the junto, and William was in the process of constructing a new whig ministry when he died.

Read quickly, this account of William's role in politics at Westminster might seem little but a dizzying record of min-isterial reshuffles and royal spats with parliament. Under-neath this, however, there was a greater significance to his actions. The king's prioritization of the struggle against Louis in Europe meant that he was willing to accept changes in England which earlier kings would not have entertained. Lacking any real interest in English politics beyond the need to maintain the country's willingness to face France, the king gave up powers to parliament which the monarchy had long resisted surrendering, and showed an absence of personal grudges or favouritism unprecedented in the Stuart dynasty.

As a result William's actions in the 1690s remodelled the constitution and the political process, perhaps more completely than the revolution of 1688. By 1702 the king's determination to avoid fights with his legislature which might disrupt the war effort had handed over key elements of the prerogative, including control of royal expenditure and of the size of the army, and the right to call and dissolve parliament at will. Similarly, the king's willingness to work with any team of ministers who would lead the struggle against Louis had done much to regularize factional struggle into a working party system. Once it was clear William would not use the court's power to attack political opponents, and would always be looking for alternative parties which might be more effective in government, the rules of political engagement changed. The route to power no longer lay through dominating the royal court and hoping to use it to destroy enemies. Rather, it became the responsible demonstration that a party could provide more effective administration than its rivals, that it was better able to manage the parliaments which could scupper that project, and therefore that it had built political alliances and won elections. In these ways a foreign king with foreign priorities broke the cycle of political instability into which England had fallen in the seventeenth century. Once there was a king whose main attention was focused outside the realm, monarchy found ways to work with legislators, and parties found more peaceful ways of trying to win power.

Scotland and Ireland

Once William had secured control of Scotland and Ireland his dealings with them followed a remarkably similar pattern. In both kingdoms he worked for a rapid end to any close personal involvement in order to free himself to organize the war in Flanders. His strategy for achieving this was to entrust royal policy to local politicians. He hoped that these would manage local parliaments, which in turn would provide enough appearance of consultation to secure supply and avoid any dangerous build-up of grievances. Unfortunately, however, this neat plan failed in both Scotland and Ireland—and for very similar reasons. From Dublin and Edinburgh the king's strategy looked like neglect. This was especially true as the monarch in London could not afford to offend his European allies or the Westminster legislature (as it was his greatest source of finance), and so sometimes had to sacrifice the interests of the northern and western kingdoms to placate others. As a result the 1690s saw growing hostility to William's rule. In both Scotland and Ireland, factional enemies of the king's ministers took up a 'country' rhetoric which accused administrations of absolutism, corruption, and bowing to England's demands.

This pattern emerged in Scotland as early as 1689. Then, William's attempts to fend off the claim of right and articles of grievance had been weakened by the structural difficulties of Scottish politics. The central problem was that the country was divided into many bitterly opposed factions. As a result, when the king appointed a minister to a plum job, all that person's rivals would be alienated. They would band together in parliamentary opposition and would garner support by adopting a country position. Exactly this happened to the king's first lord high commissioner, William Hamilton, duke of Hamilton. As Hamilton tried to preserve the royal prerogative over the summer of 1689, his enemies coalesced into the 'Club' which denied supply until the demands of the claim and articles were met. The king solved this difficulty by dismissing Hamilton and appointing George Melville, Lord Melville, to offer concessions in 1690, but this obviously left the danger that a similar train of events would occur every time a chief minister was appointed. In the early 1690s the nightmare was realized. The king had to give up successive servants when they were attacked for mishandling religious tensions, for their parts in the Glencoe massacre, or for their toadying to an English-dominated court. One possible solution to this instability, circulating within the Edinburgh administration from the winter of 1689–90, was that William go to Scotland himself to flatter the faction leaders. This, however, was never attempted. The king's attentions were always directed towards securing victory on the battlefields of Ireland and Flanders, and on pleasing the purse-carrying Westminster Commons, and he was determined not to be distracted from these arenas by affairs in Edinburgh. Nothing, therefore, stemmed factional skulduggery or the growth of anti-English, anti-Williamite, and country sentiments.

William's problems in holding his northern kingdom were neatly encapsulated by the controversy surrounding the Company of Scotland. This body was founded in 1695 to allow Scots to trade overseas, but as it pursued its commercial expansion, and especially when it launched a plan for a commercial colony on the Darien isthmus in Central

America, William was forced to oppose it. The English Commons protested against commercial competition from Scotland, while the Darien scheme outraged the king's Spanish allies, on whose territories the colony would be illegally planted. Consequently William sacrificed his Scottish subjects in order to pursue his conflict with Louis XIV. In 1695 he sacked the ministers who had approved the foundation of the company, muttering he had been 'ill-served' in Scotland (Riley, 99). Later he thwarted the company's attempt to raise money on European stock markets by informing investors in Hamburg that it was 'an Affront to his Royal Authority' (*Memorial Given*), and in 1699 he ordered his governor in Jamaica to give no aid to the Darien colonists, with the result that the settlement was a disastrous failure. Reaction in Edinburgh was predictable. Popular anti-English sentiment grew and factional enemies of the new high commissioner, James Douglas, second duke of Queensberry, exploited it. Consequently William faced a series of stormy parliamentary sessions between 1698 and 1701, in which supply was in constant danger and in which Queensberry maintained control only by massive use of patronage and strategic prorogations.

Ireland too was a scene of parliamentary discontent in the 1690s. Problems here again stemmed from the priority of English and European interests in the king's mind. The first source of discontent was the treaty of Limerick. As William's commanders tried to mop up Jacobite resistance in the west of Ireland in 1691 it became clear that a long operation could only be avoided by offering generous terms to the rebels. Accordingly the king decided to free his troops for Flanders by agreeing that those Jacobites who chose not to leave for

France (and those under their protection) could keep their estates and could exercise the religious freedoms they had enjoyed under Charles II. For the Irish protestants represented in parliament, this was outrageous—the Limerick terms sacrificed their security by allowing Catholic Jacobites to live and worship unmolested, and demonstrated that the king was more interested in his European war than in loyal Irish subjects. As a result of protestant anger the legislative sessions of the 1690s ran beyond William's control. In 1692 his first parliament ended in less than a month, with only insufficient supply granted and a blow to William's diplomatic honour. One clause of the Limerick treaty had bound the king to use his 'utmost endeavour' to have it ratified, but the mood in parliament prevented his even raising the issue. The parliament of 1695 went better—but only because the lord lieutenant, Henry Capel, Baron Capel, surrendered the initiation of money bills, remained silent about Limerick, and accepted the first penal law against Catholics in contravention of the treaty's spirit. Only in 1697 did William dare ask the parliament to confirm the deal he had struck in 1691. Even then he had to accept further penal legislation, and a further erosion of his reputation when the ratification ignored earlier promises on religious freedom and the rights of those who had been under Jacobite protection.

After this session bitter new issues arose between William and his Irish protestant subjects. First, in May 1699 the Westminster legislature attempted to protect the English sheep industry by banning the import of Irish wool. William accepted the Woollens Act to placate a body in full cry against his army, even though it damaged a vital part of the Irish economy. Secondly, in April 1700 William avoided

tension in London by assenting to a resumptions act which
reconfiscated Irish estates originally forfeited by Jacobites
and subsequently granted by the king to his protestant
allies. In both cases Irish public opinion railed against English claims to legislate for Ireland. Pamphlets and petitions
implied the king had sacrificed Ireland for English gold, and
William found he dared not call his Irish parliament again
before he died.

In the end, therefore, William's handling of the legisla-
tures in Edinburgh and Dublin was far less successful than
his dealings with the assembly in Westminster. Whereas
in England the king's rule provided solutions to the structural problems of politics, in Scotland and Ireland it merely
underlined the difficulties of governing parliamentary poli-
ties at a distance. William had to rule through parliaments
in Dublin and Edinburgh because he needed supply. He
could not, however, go in person to manage them, or redress
their central grievances, because of his priorities in Flanders and Westminster. As a result local ministries merely
provoked factional rivalry to add to national and 'country'
sentiment, so that by the last years of the reign radical action
to end instability was being urged. By the late 1690s William
himself returned to urging parliamentary union between
England and Scotland, while Irish politicians debated the
merits of union or of autonomy under the crown as routes
out of political chaos.

Private man, public monarch

William and religion

William's personal faith was profound if simple. At its foundation lay a deep piety which drove him to attend prayers at least once a day, to follow regimes of close spiritual self-examination, and to share in his wife's efforts to make the English court a more godly and chapel-centred institution. Upon this firm base the king's religion rested on three principal pillars. First, he retained a basic belief in the Calvinist doctrine, plain worship, and presbyterian government of the Dutch Reformed church. William remained a practising member of that congregation whenever in the Netherlands; he was initially disappointed that his wife continued to worship according to Anglican rites and at Torbay in 1688 he asked Gilbert Burnet what that Arminian thought of Calvinist predestination now he had seen God's blessing on the prince's expedition (*Bishop Burnet's History*, ed. Burnet and Burnet, 1.789). Secondly, and notwithstanding his commitment to the Dutch form of faith, William believed that religion should never be imposed by persecution. He urged religious toleration in all the countries in which he had influence; he employed a wide range of denominations in his armies and administrative service—including even Catholics and Jews; and in 1689 he objected to a phrase in the Scottish coronation oath binding him to root out heresy until it was explained that the clause was an empty form of words. Thirdly, William had a strong sense of his providential role. Although always careful to reject the notion that heaven had sent him to conquer Europe for reformed Christianity (for example, his 1688 manifesto avoided whipping up protestant crusading sentiment), he at least believed that the deity had charged him with saving the continent from Louis XIV's brand of persecuting Catholicism. He therefore allowed his propagandists in both Holland and England to paint him as the almost millennial saviour of the faith and told the English fleet in 1688 that he was intervening to preserve their religion 'the total ruine of which in these kingdomes is designed as itt is already accomplisht in France' (Herbert).

However, while these beliefs ran deep with the stadholder-king, circumstances meant that William had to compromise them in individual situations. In particular, his overriding concern with defeating Louis ensured that he would be prepared to abandon any promotion of Dutch reformed orthodoxy, or even to dilute his commitment to toleration, if these ideals might alienate people who would otherwise join in the struggle against France. For example, William was helped to power in the United Provinces by the preaching of the pro-Orange Calvinist wing of the Dutch church. Once it became clear, however, that this alliance strengthened opposition to the stadholder among more 'liberal' Dutchmen, William reached out to other sections of spiritual opinion, and from the 1680s deliberately balanced strains of faith in his appointments. In England similarly he showed flexibility. Although his first advisers on religion were dissenting whigs who shared his commitment to toleration and advocated a Dutch-style church, William changed tack on realizing that support for dissenters antagonized the Anglican majority in his new realm. From the first, allies warned him he must make a visible commitment to the Church of England by being seen at its services. William took this advice, attending Anglican worship as early as his sojourn in Exeter in November 1688 and flattering the London clergy on arrival in the capital. A few months later he shifted even more decisively towards Anglicanism after his first intervention in English ecclesiastical politics had ended in disaster. On 16 March 1689 William appealed to the House of Commons to abandon the religious tests which kept non-Anglicans out of public office. This enraged a large group of MPs, who began to threaten the king's hold over the parliament, and forced William to abandon his dissenting allies. From March the king began taking advice on ecclesiastical affairs from the committed Anglican earl of Nottingham and, although the king's advocacy secured a limited toleration act in April, he effectively gave up hope of further concessions to nonconformity. Instead he spent the autumn flattering the established church and assuring it that its protection was his highest priority. After 1689 the king never again questioned the Test Acts; he continued to attend Anglican services regularly (even sitting through implicitly anti-Calvinist sermons), and left churchmen to run their own affairs. Until 1694 Mary—who was a loyal and pious member of the Church of England—handled ecclesiastical policy; after her death William rubber-stamped the injunctions of a commission of leading bishops.

In Scotland and Ireland, too, William's personal religious preferences were sacrificed to political priorities. In the northern kingdom William had hoped for a generous religious settlement which would satisfy his commitment to toleration, and might unite all shades of religious opinion behind his rule. Once it became clear, however, that much of the Scottish episcopalian clergy had sympathies with Jacobitism, and once the country opposition began using hostility to prelates to whip up resentment against English influence, the king was forced to conciliate the rigid presbyterians. In June 1689 he gave his assent to the act abolishing episcopacy, and despite writing to the general assembly of the kirk in October 1690 asking it for 'moderation' in its dealings with the episcopal clergy (National Archives of Scotland, CH1/1/12, fol. 19), the king did nothing as non-presbyterians were investigated, condemned for scandalous conduct, and deprived.

Meanwhile, in Ireland the terms of the 1691 treaty of Limerick, granting a degree of religious freedom to Catholics, clearly gelled with William's general determination not to persecute. Once again, however, the king had to bend to political circumstance. As the Irish parliament expressed its opposition to any generous settlement with papists, William was forced to give way simply to retain any influence in the Dublin Commons. In 1695 he assented to an act disarming Catholics and forbidding them to own horses worth more than £5 or to send their children abroad for education. Two years later he accepted a bill banishing both the regular clergy and Catholic 'dignitaries' (a category which included bishops), and was forced to abandon the grant of religious freedom when the treaty of Limerick was ratified. Overall, therefore, William's political needs meant that he had limited opportunity to shape his realms according to his religious convictions, and forced him to be a rather different spiritual head in his various realms. A tolerant but committed member of the reformed church in the United Provinces, he became a pious Anglican in England, accepted a rigid presbyterian settlement in Scotland, and put his name to a penal code of intolerant legislation in his westernmost realm.

Marriage and sexuality

William's union with Mary in London in 1677 was a political convenience. The prince had pursued it in hopes of gaining influence over English foreign policy, and had not formed any deep attachment to his fifteen-year-old bride. Predictably, therefore, the early years of the marriage passed with little emotional commitment from the prince. Within a short time of his return to The Hague, one of Mary's maids of honour, Elizabeth Villiers, may have 'intercepted his favour' sufficiently to become his mistress (*Dictionary of National Biography*, 1900), and a further wedge was driven between the prince and his wife by his suspicion that she hoped to exercise the plenitude of royal power if she ever came to the throne in Britain. Mary's miscarriages in 1678 and 1679 also meant there were no children to cement bonds between the couple.

Yet despite this dreadful start the marriage was ultimately a success. Mary fell deeply in love with William soon after

the wedding, and after the princess confronted her husband about his relationship with Villiers in 1685 the prince
became more discreet about his affair. Also, some time in
1686, Gilbert Burnet seems to have corrected William's mis-
conceptions about Mary's political ambitions. After talking
to the princess Burnet was able to tell her husband that
she would resign all effective power to him were she ever
to become queen of England. With such stumbling blocks
removed the way to an effective partnership was clear.
During his invasion of England William may have been
careful to keep Mary out of the country until he was in
control and she could not form an alternative focus for anti-
Jacobite feeling, but he soon came to recognize her value in
helping hold his new realm and quickly invited her to join
him.

As the biography of Mary in this volume makes clear,
William's wife could perform a large number of useful func-
tions for the regime. The fact that Mary was English, and
was the daughter of the displaced king, helped to ease local
scruples about accepting a foreign monarch with a rela-
tively weak hereditary claim. The queen also soothed fears
about the fate of the Church of England under William, and
rapidly proved an asset in the field of public relations. Her
open character helped her husband build a welcoming court;
her piety enabled him to construct an image of a godly royal
household; and her active attempts to present the monarchy
as an engine of moral reform served as a centrepiece of
government propaganda. Finally, Mary proved useful during
William's absences in Ireland and Flanders in the early
1690s. Although the queen was reluctant to take up executive responsibilities, she was the obvious person to govern

while the king was abroad and she guided England through successive difficult summers between 1690 and 1694. In these periods her loyalty to her husband, and especially her refusal to take any but urgent decisions before consulting him by letter, ensured continuity. Such steadfast service eventually had personal as well as political consequences. When Mary died from smallpox on 28 December 1694 it became clear how attached her husband had become to her. For nearly a month he was inconsolable, and he organized an impressive funeral. His grief was well placed. It is arguable that the increasing difficulty William found in preserving support for his policies after 1695 stemmed from the loss of his popular consort.

Outside his marriage William's sexuality was, and has remained, controversial. It is probable that Elizabeth Villiers continued as his mistress until Mary's death, at which point she was put aside. The king—counselled by an admonitory Archbishop Thomas Tenison—came to believe that the queen's loss was a punishment for his sins, and resolved to amend his personal life. What has been far less clear is the nature of his relationship with his two closest friends. Jacobite propaganda, and much contemporary gossip, accused William of homosexual liaisons—first with Hans Willem Bentinck (who was made earl of Portland once in England), and after 1695 with the handsome courtier Arnold Joost van Keppel, who seems to have displaced Portland in William's affections. Historians will probably never know the truth of these accusations. It can be said that William was very close to both men and frequently stayed up late into the night with them. It is also true that the king's apartments interconnected with his friends' during their successive periods of favour, and that Portland wrote to William in 1697 telling him he must break with Keppel because his behaviour was fuelling allegations of unnatural vice (Japikse, 1.1.198–9).

However, there are other explanations for the relationships. Portland had been a long-standing ally of the prince, whose wife William enquired about with affection. Keppel was a faithful servant who shared the king's passions for hunting and warfare. As for the other evidence: interconnecting apartments were appropriate for men who served as the king's private secretaries; Portland's letter can be put down to jealousy of a factional rival; and other parts of the case such as Burnet's reference to a secret royal vice 'of one sort' (*Bishop Burnet's History*, ed. Burnet and Burnet, 1.439), or supposedly homoerotic ceiling decorations in the king's bedchamber at Hampton Court (Antonio Verrio's *Endymion in the Arms of Morpheus* in the great bedchamber), are highly circumstantial. Thus although the argument is not proved that the king was too busy dictating letters late in the evenings to engage in same-sex affairs (Baxter, *William III*, 352), nor is there clear evidence that he ever did get involved in them. The most important thing about William's private life remained his close relationship with his wife. Without Mary's support in presenting the new regime, the king would have met with less success.

William's royal style

Comparing William's style of kingship to that of his recent predecessors it would be easy to argue that 1688 marked a revolution in the image of monarchy at least as profound as that in its prerogative power. William had ideological reasons for scaling down monarchical splendour which might suggest he was consciously working towards a plain, perhaps even bourgeois, style of kingship. He was from the Netherlands, a republic which had rejected regal magnificence; he was aware that the English had just reacted against a Stuart dynasty they suspected of self-aggrandizement; and he wished to distance himself from Louis XIV, a man whose public image was marked by glorifications of his absolute power. Added to this was the personal reticence which made William reluctant to act as the focus of a glittering court life. Never a socialite, the king was uncomfortable among the English (a nation whose mores and sense of humour he never quite fathomed); he found life in smoky London unbearable because of a respiratory complaint; and his favoured pastimes—hunting, art connoisseurship, and adultery—he pursued with only a few close companions.

The impact of all these influences on the presentation of monarchy were noticeable. After 1688 there was less glitter surrounding the ruler; there was less sense that the court was the cultural and social centre of the realm; and there was less grandiose suggestion of the semi-divinity of the king. For example, William abandoned the practice of touching for scrofula. This ceremony, which had suggested the miraculous powers of monarchs to cure disease, was particularly unsuitable for a post-revolutionary ruler. Similarly, William stressed his service to the nation in every public statement. His speeches, especially those to parliament, were full of deference to legislators, promising them from the first that he would 'never do any thing that may lessen your good opinion of me' (*Journals of the House of Lords*, 14, 1685–1691, 128).

Again, monarchical extravagance was scaled down. The king lived for much of his reign in the domestic suites he built for himself at Kensington and Hampton Court, rather than entertaining lavishly at Whitehall, and his propaganda stressed the taxpayers' money was used for national defence, not on 'sumptuous Palaces' (*Short Reflections*, 25). Major projects to enhance monarchy were rejected as too expensive or too absolutist in style. Sir Christopher Wren's blueprints for wholesale redevelopment at Hampton Court (in 1689) and Whitehall (in 1698 after the old palace was destroyed by fire) were never adopted, and this left Greenwich Hospital, which was for the use of naval heroes rather than the king, the most impressive architectural achievement of the day. In fact, so pinched was William's style of rule that it began to occasion critical comment. Retreat from a visible court in Westminster to isolated rural seats fed rumours of homosexuality and entrapment by evil counsellors (Sir Charles Sedley told the Commons that courtiers kept the king at Kensington 'as in a box' (*Parliamentary Diary of Narcissus Luttrell*, 55)), while close advisers became worried that the king was harming himself by his lack of spectacle, visibility, and social grace. In 1689 Burnet complained to William's face that he was too reserved and private for his new subjects. When cut off by the monarch, he immediately retired to his closet to finish his observations by letter: the incident cooled relations between the two men for several months (Bodleian Library, Oxford, MS Add. D.24, fol. 211).

Yet for all that has been said, it would be a mistake to portray William as rejecting regal grandeur completely. The United Provinces may have been a republic but the Orange family were hereditary princes who had married repeatedly into royalty, and who had maintained courtly magnificence and regal distinction from the rest of the Dutch population. It was unlikely, therefore, that William would utterly abjure personal grandeur. In the Netherlands he insisted on ceremony and etiquette which emphasized his elevated position, and built himself an impressive—if not grandiose—house and gardens at Het Loo. In England too the new king preserved much of the majesty of 'his majesty'. For example, he reversed the cuts in the numbers of court personnel which had been made under James II, and much of the ritual life surrounding the English king was preserved. The coronation, attendance at lord mayor's shows, and triumphal celebrations after military victories were staged as lavishly as ever, and some regal ceremonial was actually expanded. The frequency of parliamentary sessions in the 1690s meant that royal openings of the legislature occurred far more regularly than ever before and the new open piety of the court meant that the monarch's daily visits to chapel became more visible affairs involving greater numbers of courtiers. Similarly, the 1694 funeral for Queen Mary—including the attendance of the entire Commons and Lords, and the draping of the funeral route with £50,000 worth of black cloth—was the largest yet staged.

Cultural magnificence, too, was not as curtailed as may have been implied. William attracted leading English artists to his court, including the musician Henry Purcell, the painter Godfrey Kneller, the architect Christopher Wren, and the woodcarver Grinling Gibbons. He also indulged his passion for connoisseurship by enhancing and displaying the Royal Collection of paintings in his residences. While under his patronage the Chapel Royal became a leading force in the production of English sermons. Again, building at Hampton Court—pushed forward under Mary in 1689–94 and renewed in 1698 after the burning of Whitehall—may have been on a smaller scale than Wren's original plans but, with a richly decorated new courtyard, was still prodigious. Outside the palace extensive gardens dominated the landscape and demonstrated the wealth of the king through elaborate parterres, 'wildernesses', and fountains. Moreover, the whole palace spoke allegorically of William's royal status and providential elevation to rule. An iconographic scheme based on Hercules, who was endlessly encountered in garden sculptures, wall decorations, and paintings, reminded viewers of William's descent from Henri IV of France (for whom Hercules had been a favoured symbol) and of the king's role as a divinely chosen godly champion. Thus, while William avoided the regal dazzle of Henry VIII, or Charles I, he nevertheless cut a more impressive figure than any 'bourgeois' monarchy would allow.

A contested legacy

7

William's death

In popular folklore William is supposed to have died after his horse tripped over a molehill. The incident for years after allowed Jacobites to toast the vanquishing creature as 'the little gentleman in black velvet'. Sadly for romance, the story is only partly true. Certainly William's horse stumbled on 21 February 1702 and the king broke a collarbone in the fall. However, he made a steady recovery from his injuries in the next couple of weeks, and was soon back conducting business, if not appearing in public. It was only on 5 March that the true cause of death—a pulmonary fever—became evident. The king collapsed after walking in the gallery of Kensington House, weakened rapidly, and became convinced on the 7th that he was dying. He died on the morning of the 8th, having been attended in his final hours by his spiritual adviser Archbishop Tenison, his close counsellor Bishop Burnet, and his still squabbling friends Keppel and Bentinck.

The privy council buried William privately in Westminster Abbey on the night of 12 April. In the British and Irish

realms he was succeeded by his sister-in-law Anne, but in
the Netherlands he was denied his wish that his cousin,
John William Frisco, stadholder of Friesland and Groningen,
inherit his political offices. The Provinces had remained
loyal to William's war policy in the 1690s but, despite earlier declarations that his position was hereditary, enough
republican sentiment remained in the Low Countries to
block any accession of a cadet branch of the Orange family.
The stadholderships of William's provinces, and the federal
military offices, were therefore left vacant. William's will
was opened in The Hague on 12 May. It bestowed a large
legacy on Keppel but gave the bulk of the personal estate to
John William Frisco.

William's subsequent reputation has been patchy, but gen-
erally muted. For centuries he has been exalted by the
protestants of Ireland. Eighteenth-century commemora-
tions of William's 1690 campaign solidified later into badges
of Ulster protestant identity and as a result the king has
been celebrated in the northern province in wall paintings,
banners, processions, and the Orange order. In Scotland,
England, and Wales, by contrast, the king has received little
honour. He has not been greatly lauded, despite exerting
himself in ways which usually earn lionization from the
British: opposing a continental threat and acting to establish a parliamentary constitution. His disappearance began
almost immediately. The monuments the privy council
planned for the king in Westminster Abbey, and in some
'public place' (Luttrell, *Brief Historical Relation*, 5.154),
were never erected, and the political nation seemed willing
to forget him under Queen Anne.

Subsequently English and Scottish commentators remained unenthusiastic. To be sure some early writers praised William greatly, especially those such as Burnet and Paul de Rapin Thoyras who had been intimately connected with his cause. After this, however, there were few Georgian panegyrics, and while Thomas Babington Macaulay made him the hero of 1688 in his youthful writings, by the time he came to write his *History of England* (1848) this worship had abated. The *History*'s William is still admirable, but it was the parliamentary politicians, finally coming to their senses in the convention, who truly laid the foundations for English greatness. In the twentieth century enthusiasm was cooled further by the sense that William had cared little for his British realms. That was the burden of the first *Dictionary of National Biography* article (1900), reinforced by G. M. Trevelyan's observation that William had come to England in 'cold judgement' of his European interests (Trevelyan, 54), and confirmed in the historiographic outburst at the tercentenary of 1688 which tended to present the revolution as a Dutch invasion (see especially Israel, 'Dutch role'). William thus went for 300 years with few champions, and the king remained a shadowy figure in British perceptions in the early twenty-first century. Public houses explicitly named after William III are vastly outnumbered by those celebrating the far less significant William IV, and the present author still has to explain who William was, when he lived, and what he got up to, when asked by non-historians what he studies.

Explaining obscurity

There are various reasons for this obscurity. Most importantly, perhaps, William's foreignness has told against him.

The British like their icons British, and the contemporary perception that the prince of Orange was loyal primarily to Holland (Queen Anne launched her reign with a ringing statement that her heart was entirely English (*Journals of the House of Lords*, 17, 1701–1704, 68)) was never fully dispelled. Similarly there may have been some embarrassment that the country had to be rescued from James II by a Netherlander. From the earliest days the revolution of 1688 was extolled as the foundation of Britain's free constitutions. However, commentators such as Edmund Burke, Macaulay, and Trevelyan tended to play down William's role in the events of 1688–9, making the revolution look less like a foreign incursion and more like an indigenous movement to settle the nation's affairs. Again, William's unpopularity towards the end of his reign may have curtailed praise at his death and prevented celebration taking root.

By 1702 gratitude at his actions against an ambitious Catholic king had been replaced by resentment at tax burdens, and this resentment lived on in the national memory. Paradoxically also, attempts to celebrate the stadholder-king may have helped to submerge him. In Ireland a special day—the anniversary of the Boyne—was given over to remembering the Orange legacy. As a result it passed into popular culture. In England by contrast, the thanksgiving for William's arrival was piggy-backed onto the 5 November pyrotechnics marking the discovery of Guy Fawkes's plot. This move was justified on the ground that the prince's landing at Torbay had occurred on the anniversary of the discovery of the gunpowder treason, and was supposed to magnify William by fitting him into a grand providential plan. In practice, however, it told against celebration. Memory of the Dutchman was lost in the established excitement of exploding effigies of Fawkes.

Other important explanations for William's unpopularity centre on his personality. Those close to the king (Bentinck, Keppel, Dijkvelt, Fagel, Heinsius, Tenison, Mary) were very close indeed, and he elicited great loyalty from them. Beyond this inner circle, however, the king had traits which made it hard for contemporaries to warm to him, and have not endeared him to subsequent generations. Most obviously, he was a monomaniac. The defeat of Louis gripped him his whole adult life, and took him away from his British subjects. Instead of appearing among, or trying to charm, his people, William spent much of his life in sieges of Flemish towns or in hours of diplomatic correspondence. Compounding this obsession was a multifaceted lack of sociability. William detested all frivolity. He did not suffer fools at all. He accepted contradiction of his opinion only with bad grace, and kept a small group of intimates to which outsiders could not gain easy access. Above all, he was cold and taciturn. Burnet, who ultimately despaired of correcting this flaw in his master's personality, commented that he 'took little pains to gain the affections of the nation', and that 'his silence, when he admitted any to an audience, distasted them as much as if they had been denied it' (*Bishop Burnet's History*, ed. Burnet and Burnet, 2.85). The only cracks in the austere facade came on the occasions when William got drunk. Then, unfortunately, he was as likely to disgrace himself with wild behaviour as impress with alcohol-induced conviviality, and it has been said his inebriety was a 'dark, moody thing' (Kenyon, *Stuarts*, 185).

Even William's health and appearance told against him. He was not a fit man. In 1675 he had been floored by smallpox, and ever after was plagued by bouts of fever and asthma. These conditions were debilitating enough in themselves, but when they made it still less likely that William would join in court hospitality, and increased his preference for rural retreats, they added to the damage done by his social reticence. Nor was the king's physical presence inspiring. Despite thick brown hair (which in his youth allowed him to follow fashions without resorting to wigs), and a striking roman nose which made him instantly recognizable on coins, paintings, and prints, he was not an imposing or impressive figure. Almost diminutively short, he was not conventionally handsome, and his illnesses rendered him pale and thin. Taken together, these features made it improbable that any cult would grow round the man.

Alongside these physical and social failings were political traits which alienated his subjects. Most importantly, William's personal aloofness was often matched by arrogance about his position. Although the stadholder-king was frequently politically flexible—especially in the face of representative assemblies—he also tended to stand on his dignity. He had a keen sense of the prerogatives of his offices, and of the rights of the Orange and Stuart families, and would often compromise these only once bitter struggle had convinced him there was no alternative. Thus William's early high-handedness in the United Provinces was ended only by the overwhelming opposition it provoked, while in Britain the king's initial instincts seemed more absolutist than parliamentarian. In the early 1680s he opposed the scheme of constitutional limitations on the monarchy which might have solved the exclusion crisis. In 1689 he fought hard to beat off parliamentary encroachments on royal power, both resisting the claim of right and articles of grievance in Scotland and trying to water down the declaration of right in England. Indeed William's conversations with the marquess of Halifax in 1689 reveal an intense irritation at the Westminster parliament's attempts to control him. He sank into a paranoid delusion that there was a republican conspiracy against him, and admitted that he would have refused to confirm the revolution's limitations on his powers had it not been for 'the condition of his affayres' (Foxcroft, 2.21). Later, in the 1690s, William's gradual surrender to the English legislature was also accompanied by tensions which threatened to erode the goodwill generated by his otherwise conciliatory attitude to parliament. Only last-minute changes of heart avoided ruptures over the place bill in 1694, and the standing army in 1698.

Of course there were excuses for the defects in William's character. He had been isolated from any affectionate family in his youth; his childhood household had been a cauldron of Orangist plotting; and he had seen his country devastated by the French in his early twenties. Perhaps, therefore, it was predictable that he would grow into a distant and driven adult. There was also much to admire in the man. He was deeply loyal to those few who made it into his close circle of friends. On the battlefield he showed an incredible courage which compensated for a lack of tactical finesse. At key points in his career—especially in 1684 in his relations with Amsterdam, in 1689 in his approach to English ecclesiastical politics, and in 1690 in Scotland—he showed a readiness to learn from political mistakes. Throughout his life he was committed to religious toleration, and the reverse side of his arrogance was a single-mindedness which kept him to his central goals and allowed him to distinguish between what was essential and what could be compromised. The problem with most of these virtues, however, was that they won few supporters. Toleration was not widely popular, and personal courage on the battlefield was sometimes at the expense of the troops. Even loyalty to friends could be dangerous. William's closeness to favourites fed British fears that he was in the pockets of foreigners, while overly lavish gifts to associates provoked Commons forfeitures of estates given away in Ireland, and damaging accusations that the king had turned Bentinck into a 'Dutch prince of Wales' by grants to him there (*Gloria Cambria*).

William reconsidered

For all these reasons the British did not take William to their hearts in his lifetime, and have not subsequently changed their opinion. Yet while the king's lack of fame is explicable, it is almost certainly unjust. There will always be historical disagreements around a person as remarkable as William, so few of whose actions can be praised without qualification, but the stadholder-king can still claim considerable achievements, which should have made him one of the greatest figures in British, and European, history. First, it is arguable he preserved Dutch independence in 1672. It is true that Holland was rescued from the French by flooding its fields, rather than by Orange strategic genius, and that the military tide turned with naval victories over the English, and the willingness of Spain and the empire to come to the United Provinces' aid. Notwithstanding this, however, William's role was vital. There was serious talk of surrender once Louis had occupied Utrecht, and it was only the prince's insistence that the Dutch must resist that gave floodwaters, battleships, and allies time to save the day. Again, and on a larger scale, the stadholder can be credited with keeping Europe free of French control. Certainly the Habsburg powers played a central part in this, and William's personal military record against Louis's commanders was poor. Yet without this leader's constant determination to build alliances against Versailles, it is likely that France would have come to dominate Britain, Germany, and Italy, and could have dictated to the Habsburgs from that position. It was, after all, William who kept the Dutch in the fight through the 1670s and 1690s; it was William who persuaded the German princes to resist pressure on the Rhine in the 1680s; it was William who took the risks of expeditions to England and Ireland; and it was William again who brought together the grand alliances of 1689 and 1701.

In Britain the last Stuart king could claim equal renown. Most traditionally, but also most controversially, William could be seen as the saviour of England's parliamentary constitution. There is little space here to articulate objections to this view. Some commentators would deny that James II had been abusing his prerogatives or that he intended to introduce absolutism, while others would point to William's continuing attachment to royal power, to the limited nature of the revolution's checks on the prerogative, or to the role of the English and Welsh themselves in establishing the new regime. Yet whatever the caveats, the stadholder-king's place among the heroes of parliamentary government seems plain. James had been pushing his rights beyond general acceptability (if not beyond all interpretations of the law); contemporary English commentators admitted that there had been no way to stop him doing this until William intervened; and—while the new king may not have welcomed restrictions on his power in 1689—he tolerated statements (such as his coronation oath) which settled many long-running constitutional disputes on parliament's side. Similarly, in the years after the revolution William continued to accept expansion of Westminster's influence. Desperate for war finance, he was the first monarch to meet his parliament for a substantive session every year. Although he protested vigorously about legislative ambition, he ultimately accepted control over the length of time parliaments could sit, and the size of his army—and he positively encouraged Commons' investigations into government finance. Taken together these developments represented a revolution in the legislature's position. Called infrequently before 1688, parliament under William became a standing, and perhaps even the central, instrument of government.

Beyond this, the stadholder-king could argue for three further achievements. First, William played a significant role in establishing religious toleration in England and Wales. Over recent decades, scholars have been moving away from the idea that the Toleration Act of 1689 encapsulated a gradually enlightening public opinion. Historians are realizing that objections to liberty of conscience remained too vigorous to suggest that persecution had become unacceptable: instead some are arguing that the Anglican monopoly was broken by royal pressure. A new king, tolerant himself, could not afford to be seen as a bigot by religiously diverse allies abroad, and insisted on relief for his non-Anglican subjects—virtually as a condition of his taking the throne.

Secondly, William set Britain on the road to great power status. His prolonged war with Louis XIV taught governments to mobilize tens of thousands of soldiers and sailors, and demanded solutions to long-standing difficulties in financing sustained military campaigns. Six years into their war with Louis the British states were employing over 100,000 people in their armed forces (nearly 2 per cent of their entire population), and were paying for them through both new types of taxation and pioneering systems of funded debt. Thus while William's predecessors had often withdrawn from conflict for lack of money or effective armed forces, his successors could rely on the experienced fighting machines and the robust structures of public finance which had been developed in the 1690s.

Finally, the stadholder-king brought a fresh approach to the handling of political rivalries, at least in England and Wales, which did much to ease those countries towards a more peaceful political system. Before 1689 the state had frequently been brought towards civil conflict by factional frustrations at rivals' monopolization of power. Under Charles I, at points in the exclusion crisis, and under James II, important political actors had been drawn into conspiracy and revolt because these seemed the only ways to dislodge 'evil counsellors' from supposedly dominating the monarch's court. After the revolution William's political style prevented such frustrations. Keeping parliament in session, he provided a forum where disagreements could be aired peacefully. Wary of becoming a prisoner of one grouping, he made it clear he would always consider the claims of opposition politicians to office. Keen to keep the support of the tax-granting Commons, he looked to work with those who could control that assembly, and so made it clear that winning parliamentary votes and elections—rather than plot or rebellion—would be the chief routes to power. One of the most remarkable features of late Stuart England and Wales was the rapid return to political stability after the disasters of the seventeenth century. William's handling of the political nation must be part of any explanation of this.

Of course William had failures. Louis XIV was still a substantial threat when he died. The Dutch king had become unpopular in the British realms. His policies had perhaps worsened relations between England and the other Stuart kingdoms. He never secured his desired toleration of faiths in all the places he ruled, and especially he had to betray the Irish Catholics to maintain control of the Dublin parliament. Yet in many other ways his contribution to British life was outstanding. For preserving the island nations from French domination, for strengthening their parliamentary traditions, for promoting freedom to worship, for establishing the fiscal-military infrastructure which would make the state a world power, and for encouraging peaceful politics, William deserves a far higher reputation than he has gained.

Sources for William

S. B. Baxter, *William III* (1966) · *Bishop Burnet's History of his own time*, ed. G. Burnet and T. Burnet, 2 vols. (1724–34) · *Correspondentie van Willem III en van Hans Willem Bentinck*, ed. N. Japikse, 5 vols. (The Hague, 1927–37) · J. Israel, *The Dutch republic: its rise, greatness and fall, 1477–1806* (1995) · C. Rose, *England in the 1690s* (1999) · *Dictionary of national biography*, 63 vols. (1885–1900), suppl., 3 vols. (1901); repr. in 22 vols. (1908–9); 10 further suppls. (1912–96); *Missing persons* (1993) · T. Claydon, *William III and the godly revolution* (1996) · *Calendar of state papers: domestic series, 1688–1702* · *Journals of the House of Lords*, 14–17 (1685–1704) · *Journals of the House of Commons*, 10–13 (1688–1702) · W. Cobbett and J. Wright, eds., *Cobbett's parliamentary history of England*, 36 vols. (1806–20) · *The acts of the parliaments of Scotland*, 12 vols. in 13 (1814–75), *1689–1702* · *An account of the ceremonial at the coronation of their most excellent majesties* (1689) · E. W. M. Balfour-Melville, ed., *An account of the proceedings of the estates in Scotland, 1689–1690*, 2 vols., Scottish History Society, 3rd ser., 46–7 (1954–5), 1–147 · *To his highness the prince of Orange: the humble address of the lord mayor, aldermen and Commons of the City of London* (1688) · A. P. Barclay, 'The impact of James II on the departments of the royal household', PhD dissertation, University of Cambridge, 1994 · S. B. Baxter, 'William III as Hercules: the political implications of court culture', *The revolution of 1688–1689: changing perspectives*, ed. L. G. Schwoerer (1992) · *Diary of the times of Charles the Second by the Honourable Henry Sidney (afterwards earl of*

Romney), ed. R. W. Blencowe, 2 vols. (1843) · [E. Bohun], *The history of the dessertion* (1689) · A. Bryant, ed., *The letters, speeches and declarations of King Charles II* (1935) · E. Burke, *Reflections on the revolution in France*, Penguin edn (1968) · G. Burnet, *A sermon preach'd in the chappel of St James…23 December 1688* (1689) · J. Carswell, *The descent on England* (1969) · J. Childs, *The British army of William III, 1689–1702* (1987) · *The correspondence of Henry Hyde, earl of Clarendon, and of his brother Laurence Hyde, earl of Rochester*, ed. S. W. Singer, 2 vols. (1828) · *Private and original correspondence of Charles Talbot, duke of Shrewsbury*, ed. W. Coxe (1821) · J. Dalrymple, *Memoirs of Great Britain and Ireland*, 2 vols. (1771–3) · *The declaration of the lords spiritual and temporal, and commons of England, concerning their grievances…with their majesties answer thereunto* (1689) · *The declaration of his highness William Henry…prince of Orange…of the reasons inducing him to appear in arms…in the Kingdome of England…* (1688) · *The form of the proceeding to the funeral of her late majesty Queen Mary II* (1695) · *A form of prayers used by his late majesty K. William III when he received the holy sacrament* (1704) · *The life and letters of Sir George Savile…first marquis of Halifax*, ed. H. C. Foxcroft, 2 (1898) · R. J. Frankle, 'The formulation of the declaration of rights', *Historical Journal*, 17 (1974), 265–79 · J. Garrett, *The triumphs of providence: the assassination plot, 1696* (1980) · *Gloria Cambria, or, The speech of a bold Briton in parliament against a Dutch prince of Wales* (1702) · O. P. Grell, J. I. Israel, and N. Tyacke, eds., *From persecution to toleration: the glorious revolution and religion in England* (1991) · *The manuscripts of the House of Lords*, 4 vols., Historical Manuscripts Commission, 17 (1887–94), vol. 3 · *The manuscripts of the House of Lords*, new ser., 12 vols. (1900–77), vol. 5 · *The manuscripts of his grace the duke of Portland*, 10 vols., Historical Manuscripts Commission, 29 (1891–1931), vols. 1–4 · K. H. D. Haley, *William of Orange and the English opposition, 1672–1674* (1953) · *His highness the prince of Orange his speech to the Scots lords and gentlemen* (1689) · *The parliamentary diary of Narcissus Luttrell, 1691–1693*, ed. H. Horwitz (1972) · H. Horwitz, *Revolution politicks: the career of Daniel Finch, second earl of Nottingham* (1968) · R. Hutton, *Charles the Second: king of England, Scotland and Ireland* (1989) · J. Israel, 'The Dutch role in the Glorious Revolution', *The Anglo-Dutch moment*, ed. J. Israel (1991), 105–62 · J. P. Kenyon, *The history men*, 2nd edn (1993) · J. P. Kenyon, *The Stuarts* (1958) · *The king's apartments, Hampton Court palace* (1994) [special issue, *Apollo* magazine] · *London's great jubilee, restor'd and perform'd on Tuesday October 29 1689* (1689) · N. Luttrell, *A brief historical relation of state affairs from September 1678 to April 1714*, 6 vols. (1857) · T. B. Macaulay, *The history of England from the accession of James II*, 5 vols. (1858–61) · W. H. L. Melville, ed., *Leven and Melville papers: letters and state papers chiefly addressed to George, earl of Melville … 1689–1691*, Bannatyne Club, 77 (1843) · *Memorial given in to the senate of the city of Hamburgh* (1697) · P. K. Monod, *Jacobitism and the English people, 1688–1788* (1989) · *An order of the lords spiritual and temporal, and commons assembled at Westminster … for a publick thanksgiving* (1689) · *A paper delivered to his highness the prince of Orange, by the commissioners sent by his majesty to treat with him. And his highness answer* (1688) · *A letter writ by Mijn Heer Fagel to Mr. James Stewart—giving an account of the prince and princess of Orange's thoughts, concerning the repeal of the test and the venal laws* (1688) · S. Pincus, 'The English nationalist revolution of 1688', *Protestantism and national identity, 1650–1850*, ed. T. Claydon and I. McBride (1998), 75–104 · *Memoirs of Sir John Reresby*, ed. A. Browning, 2nd edn, ed. M. K. Geiter and W. A. Speck (1991) · *Reflections upon our late and present proceedings in England* [1689] · P. W. J. Riley, *King William and the Scottish politicians* (1979) · G. Royse, *A sermon preached before the king at Belfast on the 14th day of June, 1690* (1691) · D. J. Roorda, 'The peace of Nijmegen', *The peace of Nijmegen, 1676–1678/79*, ed. J. A. H. Botts (Amsterdam, 1980), 17–28 · H. H. Rowen, *John de Witt: grand pensionary of Holland, 1625–1672* (Princeton, 1978) · S. Schama, *The embarrassment of riches* (1987) · L. G. Schwoerer, 'Propaganda in the revolution of 1688–9', *American Historical Review*, 82 (1977), 843–74 · J. C. Simms, *The Williamite confiscations in Ireland, 1690–1703* (1956) · *Short reflections upon the present state of affairs in England* (1691) · *Some reflections upon his highness the prince of Orange's declaration* (1688) · W. A. Speck, *The birth of Britain: a new nation 1700–1710* (1994) · *A speech to his highness, the prince of Orange* (1689) · W. Temple, *Observations upon the United Provinces of the Netherlands*, ed. G. Clark (1972) · M. A. Thomson, 'Louis XIV and William III', *English Historical Review*, 76 (1961), 37–58; repr. in *William III and Louis XIV: essays 1680–1720 by and for Mark A. Thomson*, ed. R. Hatton and J. S. Bromley (1968), 24–48 · A. Herbert, *Admiral Herbert's letter to all commanders of ships and sea-men in his majesties fleet* (1688) · J. Tillotson, *A sermon preached at Lincoln's Inn on 31st Jan 1688* (1689) · G. M. Trevelyan, *The English revolution, 1688–1689* (1938) · *A true and exact relation of the prince of Orange his publick entrance into Exeter* (1688) · [J. Whittel], *An exact diary of the late expedition of his illustrious highness, the prince of Orange* (1689) · *An act for establishing the coronation oath* (1689); repr. in L. G. Schwoerer, ed., *The revolution of 1688–1689: changing perspectives* (1992), 128–30

Mary

by W. A. Speck

Upbringing and marriage

1

Mary II (1662–1694),

queen of England, Scotland, and Ireland, was born on 30 April 1662 in St James's Palace, Westminster. She was the eldest child of James, duke of York, the future James II (1633–1701), and his first wife, Anne Hyde (1637–1671). Her maternal grandfather was Edward Hyde, first earl of Clarendon, architect of the restoration of Charles II. She was named after her aunt, Mary, princess of Orange, who had recently died. At her baptism her godparents were Prince Rupert and the duchesses of Buckingham and Ormond. These relationships identified the princess with the Stuart dynasty and its survival from her birth.

Childhood and education

Apart from a sojourn in York from 1665 to 1667, to escape the last visitation of the plague, Mary lived in the south of England until she married. The question of her education was extremely sensitive, given her father's Roman Catholicism and the fact that her mother also exhibited Catholic sympathies before her death from breast cancer in March 1671. After her mother died Mary lived at Richmond Palace, where her upbringing was entrusted to a governess, Lady Frances Villiers. To avoid any suspicions being aroused about Mary's protestantism she was educated by George Morley, bishop of Winchester, Henry Compton, bishop of London, and Edward Lake, archdeacon of Exeter, who instructed her in the principles of the Church of England, to which she became devoted.

Although she learned no Latin or Greek, she did acquire French from Pierre de Laine, who in 1667 published a grammar written for the princess. According to her teacher she was 'absolute mistress of the French tongue' (Laine, 8). Her drawing-master was the dwarf Richard Gibson, who later went with her, together with his equally diminutive wife, to the Netherlands. Among Mary's other accomplishments were playing music on the lute and the harpsichord, and dancing, at which she was so proficient that on 2 December 1674 she appeared at court in the title role of John Crowne's ballet, *Calisto, or, The Chaste Nymph*. When Crowne published it in 1675 he dedicated it to her. Another work dedicated to her was one by Basu Makin on female education published in 1673, which hailed Mary as principal among all 'Ingenious and Vertuous ladies' (Fraser, 321). 'Her Age and her Rank had denied her opportunities for much study', observed Abel Boyer in 1701, 'yet she had read the best Books in English, French and Dutch' (Maccubbin and Hamilton-Phillips, 4). She showed her own concern for education in 1693 by helping to establish the College of William and Mary in Virginia. Mary spent much of her leisure time gardening, doing needlework, and playing at cards. Her interest in gardens led her to advise on the design and planting of those of the houses she possessed through marriage in the Netherlands as princess of Orange and in England after she became queen. Thus she took part in the design of the garden at Honselaarsdijk and selected exotic plants for it, and suggested the aviary at Het Loo, Apeldoom. After 1689 she discussed with Sir Christopher Wren the planning of the gardens at Hampton Court and Kensington Palace. As for her needlework, she embroidered curtains for the bedrooms in her various residences. Her addiction to card games earned her a rebuke from her tutor Dr Lake, especially when she played on Sundays.

Mary and William

The question of Mary's marriage partner was already being openly discussed when she was only eight years old. The deaths of her mother and her brother Edgar in 1671 made her second in the line of succession to the throne. In the absence of any legitimate children of Charles II, her uncle, Mary became heir to the crown after her father, James. The disposal of her hand thus became a crucial issue in British politics and European diplomacy. From the start, the claims of William of Orange (1650–1702) were pressed by protestants. William himself visited England in the winter of 1670–71 'to pretend to the Lady Mary' (*Memoirs of Sir John Reresby*, ed. A. Browning, M. K. Geiter, and W. A. Speck, 1991, 82). Although Charles II was in favour of the match, James was not, and had to be bullied into it by his brother. For a while James held off, hoping to arrange a marriage between Mary and the French dauphin. When William became stadholder in 1672 he cooled on the question, as he did not wish to identify himself with the English court and its pro-French foreign policy. With the ending of the Third Anglo-Dutch War in 1674, however, the negotiations for a marriage treaty were reopened. The earl of Danby, who was by then the chief minister in England, was particularly keen on this protestant match. Sir William Temple discussed it in a two-hour conversation with William in the Netherlands in which he enthused about the princess's eligibility. William visited England again in the autumn of 1677, when his marriage to Mary was arranged between himself and her father and uncle. She was then informed of the outcome on 21 October 1677, at which she 'wept all that afternoon and the following day' ('Diary of Dr Edward Lake', 5).

Mary's reaction was natural in an attractive young woman of fifteen when faced with the prospect of being married to the Dutchman who was so unappealing, with his blackened teeth and hooked nose, that her sister Anne called him Caliban. Mary was taller than her husband, being all of 5 feet 11 inches while he was 5 feet 6½ inches in height. She was also a passionate woman, while he was cold and regarded as unfeeling. Mary's highly emotional nature was expressed in the adolescent letters she wrote to her friend Frances Apsley, in which she described herself as the wife and her correspondent as her husband. Much of the passion she displayed can be dismissed as the excess of adolescence. The correspondents were consciously play acting, for they also signed their names Mary Clovin and Aurelia, based on characters in Philip Massinger's play *The Maid of Honour*. Nevertheless, the emotion which Mary put into her letters was very strongly expressed, in that peculiar spelling of hers

which was atrocious even by the lax standards of the time.
Thus about 1675, when she was thirteen, she wrote:

> I love you with more zeal then any lover can, I love you
> with a love that ner was known by man, I have for you
> excese of friandship more of love than any woman can for
> woman and more love then ever the constanest love had
> for his Mrs, you are loved more then can be exprest by
> your ever obedient wife vere afectionate friand humbel
> sarvant to kis the ground where one you go to be your
> dog in a string, your fish in a net your bird in a cage your
> humbel trout. (Bathurst, 60)

The reference to the love of a man for his mistress is one
of many in the correspondence, revealing how exposure to
the dissolute courts of Charles II and her father affected
her early impressions of married life. She once observed to
Frances that 'in tow or three years men are alwais wery of
thier wifes and look for Mrs as sone as thay can gett them'
(ibid., 51). Such youthful cynicism was a good preparation
for marriage to William, who took a mistress, Mary's friend
Elizabeth Villiers, even before two years had elapsed.

Their wedding took place at nine o'clock at night in Mary's
bedchamber on 4 November 1677. Significantly the king and
not her father gave Mary away. Charles 'was very pleasant
all the time'. Thus 'when the prince endowed her with all
his worldly goods, hee willed to put all up in her pocket,
for 'twas clear gains' ('Diary of Dr Edward Lake', 6). As
part of the settlement Mary received jewels worth £40,000
and an annual allowance of £10,000 plus £2000 a year pin
money. Sir Edmund Waller composed an epithalamium for
the occasion, which included the lines:

Not Belga's fleet (his high command)
Which triumphs where the sun does rise
Nor all the force he leads by land,
Could guard him from her conquering eyes.
(*The Poems of Edmund Waller*, ed. G. T. Drury, 2 vols.,
1893, 2.80)

The last line was especially unfortunate. Mary's eyesight
was always affected by migraine-like aching, which made
it at times impossible for her to read or write. At the same
time William was scarcely smitten by her, at least in the
early stages of their marriage which he regarded as purely
diplomatic, and treated her with indifference.

The departure of the newly married couple for the
Netherlands was delayed, initially because Mary was
reluctant to leave London where her sister Anne was ill
with smallpox at St James's Palace. They also had to stay
until the birthday of Catherine of Braganza, Charles II's
queen, was celebrated on 15 November. The celebrations
included a ball at which it was observed that William
danced only once with his wife. There was court gossip
about 'the prince's sullennesse, or clownishness, that he
took no notice of the princess at the playe and balle' ('Diary
of Dr Edward Lake', 9). The royal party left for Margate
on 19 November, Mary weeping all the morning. When
the queen tried to cheer her up by relating the similar
circumstances which attended her own nuptials, when she
had left her native land for a strange country, Mary replied
'But madam you came into England; but I am going out of
England' (ibid., 10). Contrary winds held them up, so they
made a leisurely journey to the coast by way of Canterbury.

They eventually set sail on 28 November, Mary in the *Katherine*, William in the *Mary*. The crossing was rough, and because Rotterdam was icebound they had to land at Terheyde. They went straight to Honselaarsdijk, which was to become Mary's favourite Dutch palace. On 14 December NS they ceremonially entered The Hague to a magnificent reception. Although the Dutch found her more appealing than the other Mary Stuart they had known, William's mother, her husband's insistence on strict protocol upset many of them. For William insisted that, while his wife could kiss the cheeks of noblemen's wives, she could not extend the same favour to those of the burghermasters.

Princess of Orange

Mary miscarried in spring 1678 and again a year later. After the first miscarriage her father wrote 'Pray let her be more careful of herself another time' (*Calendar of State Papers: domestic series, 1678*, 126). These miscarriages were bitter disappointments to her maternal aspirations and dynastic ambitions in the Netherlands and in Britain. She apparently never conceived again. This, together with her sister's failure to leave an heir after many pregnancies, suggests that there was a genetic problem, though whether inherited from their father, as has been suggested, or their mother is impossible to determine.

Although Mary scarcely found wedded bliss with the unfaithful William, she was able to transform some of the mock affection she had shown for Frances Apsley into real devotion to him. Thus she wrote to her friend on 3 March 1678 NS:

I supose you know the prince is gone to the Army but I am sure you can guese at the troble I am in, I am sure I coud never have thought it half so much, I thought coming out of my own contry parting with my friands and relations the greatest that ever coud as long as thay lived hapen to me but I am to be mistaken that now I find till this time I never knew sorow for what can be more cruall in the world then parting with what on loves and nott ondly comon parting but parting so as may be never to meet again to be perpetually in fear for god knows when I may see him or wethere he is nott now at this instant in a batell. (Bathurst, 88–9)

Mary's pining for her absent husband might have been inspired as much by loneliness as by love. For her life in the Netherlands appears to have been very solitary. Although she moved around her husband's palaces—Dieren, Honselaarsdijk, Hoofdyke, the House in the Wood, and, when it was eventually built in the 1680s, Het Loo—she was not invited to other people's residences. This could have been partly her fault, since she seems to have felt that as a princess her status was so far above the Dutch regents that she could not accept invitations. Consequently her existence was spent in card playing, needlework, and religious devotions. This pattern was only occasionally disturbed by visits, such as that which her stepmother and sister paid her in October 1678, followed by her father in February 1679, and all three in September 1679. Mary got on well with Mary of Modena while she was duchess of York. In their correspondence the duchess addressed the princess as 'the lemon', by contrast with the prince or 'the orange'. Anne's visits were also very welcome. James's second visit was to be the last time he was in the presence of his daughter. Otherwise her routine was mundane. As the author of 'The character of . . . Queen Mary II' observed of her regular practice when she returned to England, it repeated a pattern established in the Netherlands:

> What an enemy she was to idleness, even in Ladies, those who had the Honor to serve her, are living witnesses. It is well known how great a part of the Day they were employed at their needles . . . the Queen herself, when more important business would give her leave, working with them. And that their minds might be well employed at the same time it was her custom to order one to read to them while they were at work either Divinity or some profitable History. (*The Royal Diary*, 8)

Her time was also employed in purchasing jewellery, perfume, porcelain, silks, and other luxury fabrics. She became quite concerned about her extravagance, struggling vainly to reduce her expenses to some kind of order. 'I beg ye Prince to pardon . . . my mistakes', she wrote in her account book in December 1687, 'if he happens to look over this book after my death' (Walker, 322). As an early biographer noted:

> the course of her life in her Court abroad (being indeed all little else but one unvaried scene) affords but little matter of particular memoirs worthy a peculiar relation; there happened nothing of importance or weight . . . till the death of . . . Charles the second. (Laine, 49)

Religion and revolution

2

'True judgement, and a good mind'

At the time of Charles II's death in February 1685 Mary and her husband were entertaining the king's illegitimate son, the duke of Monmouth, at The Hague. Monmouth relieved the tedium of Mary's life in the Netherlands, attending magnificent balls and skating with the princess on the ice. One of the first communications from her father, now James II, which Mary received was a polite request to dismiss Monmouth from court. The duke went off to raise his fatal rebellion in England. In 1686 the scholar and future bishop of Salisbury, Gilbert Burnet, took refuge from James II in the Netherlands and was kindly received by Mary and William, who invited him to their court. There he found that:

> she knew little of our affairs till I was admitted to wait on her. And I began to lay before her the state of our court, and the intrigues in it, ever since the restoration: which she received with great satisfaction, and shewed true judgment, and a good mind, in all the reflections that she made. (*Bishop Burnet's History*, 3.134)

Burnet claimed that, until he pointed it out, Mary was ignorant of the fact that, if she became queen, William would not be king. She expressed surprise and asked him to propose an alternative, which led him to suggest that she should give her husband the real authority and try to get it legally invested in him. Although Burnet insisted that it was his own idea, and that 'no person living had moved me in it', the earl of Dartmouth, when he glossed this passage, took it for granted 'that the prince ordered him to propose it to the princess before he would engage in the attempt upon England: and she must understand it so' (*Bishop Burnet's History*, 3.138–9).

Mary appears to have become more concerned about the state of affairs in England following Burnet's account of them. Thus she intervened in favour of Bishop Compton of London when her father used the commission for ecclesiastical causes to suspend him from his spiritual duties. She also gave £200 to the fellows of Magdalen College, Oxford, who had been ejected for resisting James's pro-Catholic policies. When James issued the declaration of indulgence in July 1687 she endorsed her husband's objections to it. Their views were made public in *Pensionary Fagel's Letter to James Stewart* 'giving an account of the Prince and Princess of Orange's thoughts concerning the repeal of the Test and Penal Laws'. This open letter to Stewart, a Scottish presbyterian lawyer, dated from Amsterdam 4 November 1687 NS, was published in Dutch and English shortly afterwards. 'Their highnesses have often declared', Fagel wrote, 'that no Christian ought to be persecuted for his conscience'. They therefore offered 'full liberty of conscience' even to Roman Catholics. But they were not prepared to agree to the repeal of the Test Acts, which were a necessary safeguard for the Church of England.

In view of these gestures in support of that church it is surprising that James sought to convert his daughter to Catholicism. Nevertheless, in November 1687 he wrote to Mary a letter explaining why he had converted from the Anglican to the Catholic church. She replied that:

> though she had come young out of England, yet she had not left behind her either the desire of being well informed, or the means for it. She had furnished her self with books, and had those about her who might clear any doubts to her. (*Bishop Burnet's History*, 3.200)

Among the latter were her chaplains. George Hooper had accompanied her to the Netherlands in 1677. He had incurred William's wrath by insisting that Mary worshipped exclusively according to the liturgy of the Church of England, and by recommending Anglican works such as Richard Hooker's *Laws of Ecclesiastical Polity*. In 1679 he had been succeeded by Thomas Ken, whom William also disliked because he complained to the prince about the effects his infidelity were having on Mary. When Ken returned to England, where he became bishop of Bath and Wells, John Covel succeeded him from 1681 until 1685. In October 1685 Covel indiscreetly wrote to Bevil Skelton, English ambassador at The Hague, to inform him that 'the Princess's heart is ready to break; and yet she, every day, counterfeits the greatest joy...The Prince hath infallibly made her his absolute slave' (Singer, 2.165). When William was told about the contents of this letter he was so incensed that he gave Covel three hours' notice to leave the country.

William Stanley replaced him as Mary's chaplain. Burnet also acted as her spiritual adviser, for although James had demanded his removal from her presence he still influenced her, reading the king's letter and helping her to compose a reply:

> Thus...she gave him the trouble of a long account of the grounds upon which she was persuaded of the truth of her religion; in which she was so fully satisfied, that she trusted by the grace of God that she should spend the rest of her days in it. (*Bishop Burnet's History*, 3.202)

James replied with a reading list of relevant books, recommending her to discuss them with an English Jesuit, Father Morgan, who was then in The Hague. Mary undertook to read the books but not to see Morgan, on the grounds that conferences with a Jesuit would not be kept secret and that news about them would do her a great deal of harm. Mary informed her sister Anne, Bishop Compton, and (by means of her chaplain Dr Stanley) William Sancroft, archbishop of Canterbury, of her father's attempts to convert her. These included sending her the printed account of her own mother's conversion before she died. James's efforts ended when Mary protested against the recall of the English regiments from the Netherlands. She was relieved at being spared reading more devotional literature, which had taken up a good deal of her time without in any way shaking her Anglican faith.

The revolution of 1688–1689

Mary expressed her shock at the trial of the seven bishops, getting Dr Stanley to write to Archbishop Sancroft on behalf of herself and her husband 'to express their real concern for your grace and your brethren' (Strickland, 5.484). She also expressed scepticism about the birth of the prince of Wales in June 1688. Her conviction that there was 'quelque tromperie' ('some deceit') in the queen's pregnancy partly arose from her perplexity in reconciling the conviction that God would preserve the church through her, with the fact that she herself had not been blessed by providence with an heir (Bentinck, 71, 92–3). Although she ordered prayers for the prince in her chapel, she sent her sister Anne a long list of questions concerning the circumstances of Mary of Modena's pregnancy and lying-in. The first of these was 'whether the Queen desired at any time any of the Ladies ... to feel her belly, since she thought herself quick?' (Dalrymple, vol. 2, appendix, part 1, 305).

Mary became convinced that the prince was a supposititious child, and stopped the prayers for him. The thoughts that her father was capable of perpetrating such a fraud, and that humanly speaking the only way to save the church and the state in England was for her husband to dethrone him by force, afflicted her severely over the summer of 1688. She spent much of it at the newly finished palace at Het Loo, in remote Gelderland, where she was rarely disturbed by visitors. She had much time on her own, and spent it in meditation. She thanked God that her eyes were better than they had been for many years, and that she was able to read and write as well as to reflect. In September she moved to Dieren, but was still sufficiently remote in the country, and felt a spiritual tranquillity there despite the preparations that were being made by William to invade England.

Then in October Mary went to The Hague to be present at the prince's departure. William told her that if it so turned out that they never met again, she should remarry, though not to a papist—'paroles qui me percèrent le coeur' ('words which pierced my heart'; Bentinck, 80). She told him that she loved him only and could never love another. Besides, having been married so long and not been blessed with a child, she believed that was enough to prevent her ever thinking of what he proposed. She went with him to the river where he boarded the boat to take him to Briel. The thought of never seeing him again if the expedition miscarried was so terrible that it deprived her of her senses, and she sat immobile in her carriage for as long as she could still see him. A storm rendered the first embarkation abortive, and the task force had to return to port. This occasioned a second farewell which might have been anticlimactic after the first, but which Mary insisted 'm'étoit plus sensible encore que la première, et lorsqu'il me quitta, c'étoit comme si l'on m'eut arraché le coeur' ('was to me even more affecting than the first, and as he left me it was as if one had torn out my heart'; Bentinck, 86). That was the last time she saw William before she herself followed him to England the following February.

Burnet saw Mary just before the expedition left, and noted that 'she seemed to have a great load on her spirits, but to have no scruple as to the lawfulness of the design'. He urged upon her the importance of her backing William up to the hilt, since any sign of discord would be ruinous to the enterprise.

> She answered me that I need fear no such thing: if any person should attempt that, she should treat them so,

as to discourage all others from venturing on it for the future. She was very solemn and serious, and prayed God earnestly to bless and direct us. (*Bishop Burnet's History*, 3.311)

While the expedition was under way she worshipped four times a day, and the rest of the time meditated and composed prayers. When she learned that William had successfully landed she allowed herself to relax four days a week, but refrained from playing cards. She still kept herself away from the public during the weeks of the revolution in England, coming out of her self-enforced seclusion only to entertain the Elector Frederick III of Brandenburg and his wife.

One of the prayers that Mary composed was for the proceedings in the Convention which was discussing the arrangements for the disposal of the crown. The proposal that there should be a regency was the outcome she privately preferred. There was a strong party led by the earl of Danby which wanted her to be queen regnant. Danby wrote to urge her to insist on her hereditary right, claiming that her insistence would sway the Convention to declare her queen. Mary replied 'that she was the prince's wife, and never meant to be other than in subjection to him, and that she did not thank anyone for setting up for her an interest divided from that of her husband' (Strickland, 5.521).

Until her views were known, however, her supporters argued strenuously against those who wished William to be king. Thus where the latter were in favour of the view that the throne was vacant, Mary's supporters contested it on the grounds that James had forfeited the crown through his Catholicism and that all other Catholics were similarly disbarred, so that the succession went automatically to the next protestant heir, who was Mary. Had Mary been present in England, notwithstanding her own preference, this view might have gained more adherents. It certainly appears that William did not encourage her to leave the Netherlands until he was assured of the crown. He got this assurance when he indicated that he had not gone over to England to be 'his wife's gentleman usher'. On or about 3 February 1689 he held a meeting of leading politicians and told them that if Mary were to be declared queen 'he could not think of holding any thing by apron strings'. Unless he were offered the crown 'he would go back to Holland and meddle no more in their affairs'. This announcement 'helped not a little to bring the debates at Westminster to a speedy determination'. What clinched them was Mary's own wish, conveyed by Burnet, to rule jointly with her husband (*Bishop Burnet's History*, 3.395–6). The declaration of rights then proclaimed William and Mary king and queen, though it gave him the sole executive power. Mary was quite happy with this solution. 'My opinion', she wrote in her memoirs, 'has ever been that women should not meddle in government' (Doebner, 23).

Mary II

Mary finally arrived in England on 12 February 1689. Although she expressed sadness at leaving the Netherlands where she had been so happy, her cheerful deportment when she entered Whitehall was noted and condemned by many observers as not acting with due decorum. 'She ran about it, looking into every closet and conveniency, and turning up the quilts of beds, just as people do at an inn' wrote one admittedly hostile observer (*An Account of the Conduct of the Dowager Duchess of Marlborough*, 1742, 26). But even Burnet confessed he 'was one of those that censured this in my thoughts' (*Bishop Burnet's History*, 3.406). She put it down to guidance she had received from William that she should not betray any misgivings about entering a place from which her father had so recently fled. The very next day she went with William to the Banqueting House in Whitehall to assent to the declaration of rights and to accept the crown.

Their coronation took place in Westminster Abbey on 11 April. Bishop Compton of London officiated at it since ominously the archbishop of Canterbury, William Sancroft, declined on conscientious grounds. Mary herself felt scruples about the 'pomp and vanity' of the ceremony and the stress on the Anglican communion during it, which she felt arose from 'worldly considerations' (Doebner, 13). Throughout the ceremony the unprecedented nature of the dual monarchy was stressed. Thus where Mary or William would have received the crown kneeling on the steps of the altar if they had been mere consorts, both sat in specially made coronation chairs. The two sovereigns took a new form of coronation oath. Where James had sworn to confirm the laws and customs granted to the English people by his predecessors, they undertook to govern according to the statutes agreed on in parliament. Again, where their predecessor had agreed to uphold rightful customs, they took the oath to maintain the protestant religion. A medal struck to commemorate the coronation depicted William as Jove thundering against James II as Phaeton leaping out of a chariot at Jove's anathemas. But Jacobites claimed that the chariot represented Mary as the Roman matron Tullia, who had driven out Tullius to set up Tarquin, and that she was dethroning her father.

Far more devastating to Mary's peace of mind was a letter she received from her father at this time, saying that previously he:

> had wholly attributed her part in the revolution to obe-
> dience to her husband; but the act of being crowned was
> in her power, and if she were crowned while he and the
> prince of Wales were living, the curse of an outraged
> father would light upon her, as well as of that God who
> has commanded duty to parents. (Strickland, 6.9)

Jacobites kept up throughout her reign the charge that Mary had behaved unnaturally in replacing James. In June 1689 they exploited the queen's discomfiture at a production of John Dryden's *The Spanish Fryar*. The plot, involving a queen of Aragon who had usurped the throne, was grist to their mill.

> In one place, where the queen of Arragon is going to
> church in procession, tis said by a spectator, Very good, she
> usurps the throne, keeps the old king in prison and at the
> same time is praying for a blessing on her army ... Twenty
> more things are said which may be wrested to what
> they were never designed. (Dalrymple, vol. 2, appendix
> 2, 79)

In 1690 a Jacobite poem imagined her lying in bed 'at dead of night ... in her own father's lodgings at Whitehall'. The ghost of her mother draws back the curtain and upbraids her saying:

> Can quiet slumber ever close thine eyes?
> Or is thy conscience sunk too low to rise?
> From this same place was not thy aged Sire
> Compelled by midnight-summons to retire? . . .
> Had he been murdered, it had mercy shown
> 'Tis less to kill a king, than to dethrone.
> (Lord, 5.298–9)

To most of her subjects, however, Mary was more acceptable than her father or for that matter her husband, who was hated as a Dutchman and despised as an alleged homosexual. William was well aware of this, and told the marquess of Halifax in June 1689 that 'if hee left us, the Queen would governe us better' (Foxcroft, 2.222). According to Burnet, in December he came close to bringing this about:

> He thought he could not trust the tories, and he resolved he would not trust the whigs: so he fancied the tories would be true to the queen, and confide in her, though they would not in him. He therefore resolved to go over to Holland and leave the government in the queen's hands. (*Bishop Burnet's History*, 4.71)

In the event wiser counsels prevailed. Soon after the coronation in Westminster Abbey, commissioners arrived from the convention which had met in Edinburgh to offer the crown of Scotland to William and Mary. The formal ceremony was held in the Banqueting House where the king and queen accepted the claim of rights, the Scottish equivalent of the declaration of rights, and took the coronation oath. They thereby became king and queen of Scotland as well as England. Their claim to Ireland, however, was currently being disputed by James II, whose landing in Kinsale was reported to them on their coronation day in England. James was effective ruler of Ireland for over a year.

The coming of power

William's departure for Ireland in June 1690 raised the problem of the arrangements to be made for the governing of the country in his absence. At first he did not want to leave Mary in charge at all, preferring to appoint a council which would simply report to her but be answerable to himself. Thus he told Halifax that 'there must be a Councell to governe in his absence, and that the Queen was not to meddle' (Foxcroft, 2.246). However, he was persuaded that it was most convenient to pass an act of parliament vesting the administration in Mary. The Regency Act stated that, notwithstanding the Bill of Rights:

> whensoever and so often as it shall happen that his Majesty shall be absent out of this realm of England it shall and may be lawful for the Queen's Majesty to exercise and administer the regal power and government of the kingdom. (*Statutes of the Realm*, 11 vols., 1810–28, 6.170)

Some members of parliament objected to the arrangement. As one put it 'if the king should die in this expedition and the queen be regent, what if, out of duty to her father, if he land she should not oppose him?' 'The question is', riposted another, 'whether you will trust the government in the queen's hands or not at all?' Such arguments were set aside when it became clear that 'the king is resolved to trust

Mary was anxious that she 'should not make a foolish figure in the world' when she took on her new responsibilities (Doebner, 23). For much of 1689 after the coronation she had devoted herself to the same kind of interests she had cultivated in the Netherlands. Thus she had brought her collection of Chinese porcelain to Hampton Court where the royal couple spent the summer. In the autumn they had moved nearer to London to Holland House, and just before Christmas acquired Kensington Palace. Mary herself remarked on the difference between the tranquillity she had enjoyed in the Netherlands and the bustle which surrounded her in England: 'et ce qui m'afflige' she wrote to Mademoiselle la Baronne de Wassenaer d'Obdam on 10 August 1689, 'c'est le peu d'apparence que je voie d'estre encore si heureuse' ('what afflicts me is the small prospect I see of ever being so happy again'; Bentinck, 119).

The major disturbance to Mary's domestic peace had been a disagreement with her sister over Anne's intrigues with members of parliament to get a financial settlement for herself. This was the first round in a quarrel which was to estrange Mary from Anne completely. Mary thought that her sister should be content to depend on herself and her husband for her finances. But Anne, who had agreed to set aside her hereditary claim to the throne in William's favour, thought that an adequate parliamentary grant was a fair compensation, especially since she was in financial difficulties. The matter came to a head in the House of Commons in December, when Anne's supporters voted her an annual allowance of £50,000, much to Mary's chagrin. On 3 March 1690 she observed privately that there was a Jacobite party and a republican party in England, 'et que j'ay raison de craindre que ma soeur en forme une troisieme' ('and that I have reason to fear that my sister is forming a third'; Bentinck, 95). Apart from this foray into public affairs, however, Mary had been very much left at leisure to pursue her hobbies of gardening and needlework. As Burnet observed, 'she seemed to employ her time and thoughts in any thing rather than matters of state' (*Bishop Burnet's History*, 4.87). Now, however, she had to take over the government of the country.

Queen regnant

3

'In all respects heroical'

Mary was not left alone to govern, for although the Regency Act made no mention of a council, William appointed one consisting of nine of the principal ministers of state. He clearly gave her his opinion of them, for in July she wrote to him 'I thought you had given me wrong characters of men, but now I see they answer my expectation of being as little of a mind as a body' (Dalrymple, vol. 2, appendix, part 2, 143). Their failure to arrive at a consensus was due to the fact that five were tories while four were whigs. Mary was not impressed by any of the nine, her own comments on each of them being negative. Of Thomas Osborne, marquess of Carmarthen, whom William had particularly recommended to her, she wrote that he was 'of a temper I can never like'. The earl of Devonshire she found 'weak and obstinate', the earl of Dorset was too lazy, the earls of Monmouth and Pembroke were 'mad', the earls of Marlborough and Nottingham were untrustworthy, while Sir John Lowther was 'a very honest but weak man'. The ninth, Edward Russell, though he 'was recommended to me for sincerity...had his faults' (Doebner, 29–30).

Mary's inexperience in affairs of state showed in her dealings with the council, who were not overimpressed by her abilities. She confessed to William that 'as I do not know when I ought to speak and when not, I am as silent as can be'. 'Every one sees how little I know of business and therefore will be apt to do as much as they can' she further informed him. 'I find they meet often at the Secretary's [Nottingham's] office, and do not take much pains to give me an account' (Dalrymple, vol. 2, appendix, part 2, 119, 121). She soon demonstrated that they had underestimated her. Carmarthen, who held the post of president of the council, felt he should have the prevailing influence. One Jacobite libel asserted that 'she's governed in Council by the marquis [of] Carmarthen' (Lord, 5.193). In fact Mary was quite able to divide and rule the nine. To offset the influence of Carmarthen, a tory, she made a point of cultivating the whig Edward Russell, telling him 'that I desired to see him sometime, for being a stranger to business I was afraid of being too much led or persuaded by one party'. When the whigs tried to take advantage of her by offering £200,000 if she dissolved parliament she told Monmouth, who made the offer, that she would have to consult the king about it (Dalrymple, vol. 2, appendix, part 2, 122, 141). Mary's deference to William in fact resolved a problem which had agitated debates on the Regency Bill as to the division of the executive power between them. There had been some concern about the consequences of their not seeing eye to eye. In the event this never arose because Mary was anxious to prevent it. 'That which makes me in pain', she wrote to William, 'is for fear what is done may not please you. I am sure it is my chief desire...as much as may be to act according to your mind' (Dalrymple, vol. 2, appendix, part 2, 129). She stuck by the resolution adopted at the first meeting of the nine that 'all business that will admit delay must be sent to the king that his pleasure may be known' (*Finch MSS*, 2.378).

A crisis arose during Mary's first experience of government, however, which demanded decisions which could not be referred to William. The defeat inflicted on the English fleet by the French at Beachy Head in June 1690 called for urgent action by the regents. Mary rose to the occasion. 'Heaven seems to have sent us one of the most threatening junctures that England ever saw', a newspaper claimed, 'merely to set off with the greater lustre the wisdom magnanimity and justice of a princess who has made good some people's fears and other's hopes in deserving the character of another Queen Elizabeth' (*Mercurius Reformatus, or, The New Observator*, 1 August 1690). Gilbert Burnet, who saw her every week that summer, observed that she 'shewed an extraordinary firmness…her behaviour was in all respects heroical' (*Bishop Burnet's History*, 4.98). She also kept a cool head, as the treatment of the earl of Ailesbury, a suspected Jacobite, reveals. In July she issued an order for the arrest of several Jacobites, including Ailesbury. He got his wife to communicate to the queen how mortified he was that, as a suspect on bail, he could not pay his duty to her. He recalled:

> The Queen's answer was in these very words: 'Tell my Lady of Ailesbury that I love to do good to all persons as far as I can, but more especially to her husband and his family, whom I knew so well in my youngest years…and therefore, for his sake, I will break through the common forms and direct him to come at four tomorrow afternoon.'

Ailesbury accordingly waited on 'that good and incomparable Queen' and even played cards with her, to the astonishment of her companions (*Memoirs of … Ailesbury*, 1.264–5).

The loss of the battle of Beachy Head was attributed to the misconduct of the earl of Torrington, the English admiral. Mary determined to dispense with his services and to imprison him in the Tower to await the outcome of a judicial inquiry into his actions. Fortunately the situation was saved by William's victory at the battle of the Boyne. Mary was relieved to learn that her husband had won and that her father had managed to escape unscathed. Her relief that both had been spared was expressed in the letter she wrote to the electress of Hanover. 'La conservation et la victoire d'un mary d'un côté, et la préservation de la personne d'un père de l'autre … étoit plus que je n'osois espérer' ('the conservation and the victory of a husband on one side, and the preservation of a father on the other … was more than I dared to hope'; Bentinck, 107).

The problem of replacing Torrington Mary had to resolve by herself. She had initially referred the decision to William, but the advice he gave, that Edward Russell and Richard Haddock should replace the admiral, proved abortive, for Russell declined the appointment. Mary then proposed that Haddock should serve with Sir John Ashby, a strategy endorsed by the nine members of the council. When the commissioners of the Admiralty were brought in to be informed of this, however, one of them, Sir Thomas Lee, objected that they should have been consulted earlier and invited to recommend a replacement. To this Mary replied 'then the king … could not make an admiral which the admiralty did not like?' Lee answered 'no, no more he can't' (Dalrymple, vol. 2, appendix, part 2, 147). Although in the end she got her own way, backed up by the nine, Mary discovered how much such matters were accomplished 'by partiality and faction'. As she confessed to the electress of Hanover in a letter of 14 August 'les animosités personelles, que les gens ont l'un contre l'autre, sont bien désagréables, et les partis différents sont trop difficiles à ménager pour moi' ('the personal animosities that men have for one another are disagreeable enough, and the different parties are too difficult for me to manage'; Bentinck, 107). 'When I … see what folk do here', she wrote to William, 'it grieves me too much, for Holland has really spoiled me in being kind to me' (Dalrymple, vol. 2, appendix, part 2, 3). Mary's first real experience as queen had been bruising. She was relieved when her husband returned in September and expressed himself 'very much pleased with her behaviour' (Doebner, 34).

When William left England again in January 1691, this time for the Netherlands, his previous year's absence had established a routine for the running of the country. While he was on the continent the regency council dealt with routine business and Mary coped with any crises. There was concern about the discovery of a Jacobite plot involving Lord Preston, but this was dealt with by the king when he returned briefly to England. Mary's involvement in the process was limited to an exchange with Preston's daughter, whom she found admiring a portrait of James II at Kensington and asked her why she did so. The young girl answered 'I am reflecting how hard it is that my father should be put to death for loving your father' (Dalrymple, 1.466–7). The only alarm the queen faced was a disastrous fire at Whitehall, which destroyed much of the palace, and forced her to escape in her nightdress, just before the king returned in April. Otherwise Mary was able to pass her time in public playing cards and arranging a ball for her sister's birthday, and in private meditating that God would bring success to their undertakings. These meditations were not just for the blessing of providence in general, but for particular enterprises. Thus she asked God to:

> Regarde avec un oeil de compassion ceux qui sont en Irlande, et, si c'est ta volonté, mets fin à cette malheureuse guerre. Bénis pour cette fin les efforts de notre général, Mr de Ginkle, et les autres qui sont employé à cet oeuvre. (Regard with a compassionate eye those who are in Ireland, and, if it is Thy will, put an end to this unhappy war. Bless for this end the efforts of our general, Mr van Ginkel, and the others who are employed in this work. Bentinck, 101)

'The only thing of business' she dealt with, according to her memoirs, 'was the filling the Bishoprics' (Doebner, 37). The bishoprics which had to be filled were those occupied by the nonjurors, who had been deprived of their sees for not swearing oaths of allegiance to William and Mary. Burnet maintained that 'the king left the matters of the church wholly in the queen's hands' (*Bishop Burnet's History*, 4.211). But that was not always the case. 'The Queen shall give no bishoprics', William informed Lord Halifax on the eve of his first departure in 1690 (Foxcroft, 2.251). When Canterbury became vacant in 1694 on Tillotson's death, he translated Thomas Tenison to it, whereas she would have preferred Edward Stillingfleet (*Bishop Burnet's History*, 4.244).

The sensitive business of depriving Archbishop Sancroft and other nonjuring bishops, however, he did leave to his wife. She handled it admirably, choosing John Tillotson as Sancroft's replacement at Canterbury in 1691. Tillotson was just the man to lead the Church of England during the troubled years following the revolution of 1688. 'Had it been put to a poll', William Sherlock claimed, 'there had been vast odds on his side that he would have been voted into the see of Canterbury' (Sherlock, 17). Mary was even prepared to risk offending her husband by promoting George Hooper to the deanery of Canterbury, for William had expressed his dislike of the new dean. Hooper had apparently said that 'if her husband retained his throne it would be by her skill and talents for governing' (Strickland, 6.62).

Mary and Anne

Relations between Mary and her sister Anne continued to deteriorate over the summer of 1691. This time they involved perceived slights to Anne's husband, George, prince of Denmark. George had already felt insulted by the king, whom he had accompanied to Ireland the previous year. William virtually took no notice of his brother-in-law, ignoring his part in the battle of the Boyne. To the insult offered to George's military prowess the king added another relating to his naval expertise. George told William that he wished to join the navy as a volunteer, an ambition the king did nothing to curb before his own departure in January 1691. He gave orders to Mary, however, that the prince was not to be allowed to serve, and she had the invidious task in May of sending Lord Nottingham to George with orders forbidding him to join a ship to which he had already consigned his baggage, which had to be removed. The upshot was, according to a contemporary report, that 'the two sisters quarreled terribly' (Gregg, 80).

They were to quarrel even more fiercely when William returned from the campaign in October 1691 complaining about the conduct of the earl of Marlborough, Anne's favourite. The king accused Marlborough of corresponding with the exiled James II and of conniving with his wife to alienate Anne from her sister and himself. Certainly John and Sarah Churchill, the earl and countess of Marlborough, were Anne's most intimate confidants in her dispute with William and Mary. Their intrigues, which did indeed include correspondence with James, led William to cashier the earl from all his offices and to ban him from court in January 1692. Although the ban undoubtedly extended to Marlborough's wife, Anne provocatively took Sarah to court at Kensington Palace on 4 February.

Mary restrained herself from remonstrating with her sister at the time, on the grounds of the princess's pregnancy. But she wrote to her the very next morning to complain that she had 'all the reason imaginable to look upon your bringing her as the strangest thing that ever was done' (Strickland, 5.344–6). She concluded by virtually ordering Anne to dispense with Sarah's services. When Anne refused Mary evicted her from her apartment at the Cockpit. Before quitting the Cockpit, Anne sought an interview with her sister who, according to Sarah, 'was as insensible as a Statue' (Gregg, 88). Anne and Prince George moved to Syon House. In April Mary sent the earl of Rochester to Anne to demand the immediate dismissal of Sarah, upon which the princess and her husband could be reinstated in their former residence. Anne gave the spirited reply that she was quite content with her new abode, so much so 'that should the Monsters grow good natured and endulge her in everything she could desire...she would be hardly persuaded to leave her retirement' (Gregg, 90). William had become a monster, 'Caliban', the 'Dutch abortion', to the princess before this. Now Mary was identified with him in Anne's eyes. Mary attempted a reconciliation with her sister by visiting her after she had given birth to a stillborn child on 17 April. But her insistence on the dismissal of Sarah made the attempt futile. It was the last time that the sisters met. Mary made the breach permanent by issuing an order that nobody could appear at court who had visited Anne. She even forbade the mayor of Bath to receive the princess, though when she did so, according to the earl of Nottingham, she 'could not refrain from tears, and said "Thus it becomes a Queen to act, but I cannot forget she is my sister"' (Gregg, 96).

'Blessings of peace at home'

Mary was again queen regnant under the terms of the Regency Act when William was out of the country from 5 March to 18 October 1692. She appears to have been more reluctant than before to take decisions without reference to the king. Perhaps he had criticized her for some of those she had taken the previous year, possibly concerning the replacing of the nonjurors. Or it could be that she was reprimanded for her initial flippancy when she was asked to round up the usual Jacobite suspects and presented with a list headed by Ailesbury. According to him she replied that he had been arrested in 1690 for nothing, and ordered his name to be eliminated. Nottingham then replied that they had orders from the king, at which 'with warmth' Mary demanded to see his orders:

> On which the Secretary replied 'Madam we have received orders to clap up a certain number.' On which she laughed, and with life and judgement added, 'I thought persons were to be taken up for crimes and not to make up numbers as they empanel jurymen.' So other names of persons were presented to her, and finding at the top, Robert of Scarsdale, 'Stop there, my Lord. Since you will have your number, put in that Lord's name instead of my Lord Ailesbury's, and if titles please you, there is an Earl for an Earl. What is sauce for one is sauce for another.'
> (*Memoirs of ... Ailesbury*, 1.298)

If this story reached William he might not have seen the joke and instructed his wife to take his orders more seriously. At all events the earl of Nottingham noted of one decision that her advisers thought it 'very reasonable for the Queen to grant ... but her Majesty would take no resolution without the king' (*Finch MSS*, 4.40). Mary was later criticized in parliament for referring matters to William, one member expressing the wish that 'she had dispatched more herself without sending abroad for orders' (*The Parliamentary Diary of Narcissus Luttrell*, ed. H. Horwitz, 1972, 251).

There was also unease among officers of the armed forces at the disgrace of Marlborough, who spent some weeks in the Tower this year, that it was the prelude to a general purge. So seriously was this threat taken to be that Mary felt obliged to reassure naval officers:

that she reposes an entire confidence in them all, and will never think that any brave English seaman will betray her or his country to the insolent tyranny of the French, and as it is their duty and their glory to defend the government, it shall be her part to reward their service. (*Finch MSS*, 4.141–2)

This reassurance inspired sixty-four naval officers to sign an address of loyalty, pledging to venture their lives in defence of her rights and the liberty and religion of England. The navy went on to win the battle of La Hogue, and with it the command of the sea. The queen was as good as her word and rewarded the seamen with a substantial sum of money, and pledged herself to establish a hospital at Greenwich for those who were disabled. Mary might have left more to William than she needed to have done in 1692, for whatever reason; but as this episode reveals she could still rise to the occasion when it was required. Both houses of parliament recognized this when they thanked her for her administration of the government during William's absence. The Lords congratulated her on her resolute conduct 'by which the danger of an invasion was prevented and a glorious victory obtained at sea' (*Journals of the House of Lords*, 15.115). The Commons noted that while Europe was engulfed in war:

we, your Majesty's subjects under your auspicious reign, enjoyed the blessings of peace at home, and...saw your Majesty's fleet return with so complete and glorious a victory as is not to be equalled in any former age and can never be forgotten by Posterity. (*Journals of the House of Commons*, 10.698)

Although she might have treated the Jacobites leniently, Mary's feelings for her father hardened during the course of this year. When James issued a declaration on the eve of La Hogue offering vague concessions to English protestants, Mary allowed it to be published in England in order to discredit him. And when she discovered that he was involved in a plot to assassinate her husband it removed the last vestiges of respect for the former king.

Publick troubles

The following year, however, produced friction between Mary and William. Mary noted in her memoirs that her administration during his absence from 24 March to 29 October 1693 'was all along unfortunate, and whereas other years the King had almost ever approved all was done, this year he disapproved almost every thing' (Doebner, 59). The friction between them was political. Mary's attachment to the tories became stronger than ever, while William began to show a preference for the whigs. In April the queen was godmother at the baptism of the earl of Nottingham's fourteenth child. Yet the previous month, before setting out for the Netherlands, the king had appointed the whigs John Trenchard and John Somers to the second secretaryship of state and the lord keepership. The whigs in the cabinet criticized Nottingham's alleged failure to protect a merchant fleet bound for the Levant which was attacked by the French. These criticisms distressed Mary, who praised Nottingham as 'the man I found the most constant in serving the king his own way, and who was the man who really toock the most and greatest pains to do so' (Doebner, 59). Yet when William returned he dismissed Nottingham from the senior secretaryship and offered it to the whig duke of Shrewsbury. 'When I begin to reflect on this year', Mary noted at the end of 1693, 'I am almost frighted and dare hardly go on; for t'is the year I have met with more troubles as to publick matters than any other' (ibid., 58).

The following April Mary complained of infirmities which she attributed to advancing years, or to 'le chagrin et les inquiétudes qu'on a si régulièrement tous les estés' ('the grief and anxieties that I have so regularly every summer'; Bentinck, 146). It seems that Mary played less of a role as regent than usual while William was absent from 6 May to 9 November 1694. She continued to preside at meetings of the privy council, which met almost twice a week. But she rarely attended the cabinet which took the major decision to have the fleet winter in the Mediterranean in consultation solely with the king. She was thus less involved in the government of the country in 1694 than she had been in 1690. During that period, however, William had been abroad for over two and a half years, rather more than half the time. Mary had made a crucial contribution to the development of a system of governing the country during the regular absences of the king.

Mary's legacy

Reconciliation and virtue

Mary's achievement was to have reconciled the bulk of the tories to the revolution of 1688. Had William been sole ruler from the start he would have been king mainly of the whigs. Jacobitism would have had more appeal without her. It was significant that the most serious Jacobite plots against the regime took place after the queen's death. By that time, however, thanks to her most tories remained loyal to William. They accepted her as next in line to the throne after her father, conveniently dismissing her half-brother as a supposititious child. As Aphra Behn put it on Mary's arrival in England in 1689:

> The murmuring world till now divided lay,
> Vainly debating whom they shou'd Obey
> Till you great Cesar's Off-spring blest our Isle
> The differing Multitudes to Reconcile.
> (*The Works of Aphra Behn*, ed. J. Todd, 7 vols., 1992–6, 1.307)

Mary reconciled herself to the revolution by attributing it to providence. God had weighed her father in the balance and found him wanting. She and her husband were therefore the instruments of divine judgment. As Gilbert Burnet recorded, she was fully convinced 'that God had conducted her by an immediate hand and that she was raised up to preserve that Religion which was then everywhere in its last Agonies' (Burnet, *Essay*, 95). Mary's belief in providence was absolute. 'I cannot tell, if it should be his will to suffer you to come to harm for our sins', she wrote privately to William in Ireland, 'for though God is able, yet many times he punishes the sins of a nation as it seems good in his sight' (Dalrymple, vol. 2, appendix, part 2, 130). The outcome of the battle of the Boyne was a clear sign that providence still blessed their cause. But if the English mocked it by continuing in their sinful ways, providence would condemn it.

What was needed to ensure the permanence of the revolution of 1688 was a moral revolution. To inspire this Mary set an example of piety and devotion. Services in royal chapels became more frequent and more public. She surrounded herself with clergymen who had been foremost in the campaign against popery and vice under her father and her uncle. She publicized their sermons by having many which were preached before her printed. Thus where under Charles II a mere three a year had appeared by command of the king, an annual average of seventeen sermons were published by Mary's command. After her death the average commissioned by the court dropped to four a year. Preaching a sermon on the occasion of her demise Thomas Manningham noted that:

Tis to the Queen that we owe many of those Pious Treatises which have been lately Publish'd amongst us; And that multitude of plain, useful and Practical Sermons, which she approv'd of, and caused to be printed, are Her Gift to the Publick. (Claydon, 98)

Her efforts to promote piety included schemes to eliminate pluralism and non-residence in the Church of England by putting pressure on clergymen guilty of these practices 'when not enforced by real necessity' to abandon those livings where they were not resident. Just before her death she admitted that 'she had no great hope of mending matters, yet she was resolved to go on' (*The Royal Diary*, 5).

Besides setting an example at court, Mary also supported the societies for reformation of manners in their efforts to get the country to mend its ways in order to avert God's wrath. In July 1691 she issued a proclamation to the justices of the peace for Middlesex for the suppressing of profaneness and debauchery. The following year 'the queen, in the king's absence, gave orders to execute the laws against drunkeness, swearing and the profanation of the Lord's day; and sent directions over England to all magistrates to do their duty in executing them' (*Bishop Burnet's History*, 4.181–2). Some of the measures undertaken by the queen to prevent the profanation of Sunday provoked ridicule. Lord Dartmouth noted against this passage in Burnet's *History of my Own Time*:

There came forth at this time several puritanical regulations for observing the sabbath in London, savouring so much of John Knox's doctrine and discipline, that Burnet was thought to have been the chief contriver. One was that hackney coaches should not drive upon that day; by another, constables were ordered to take away pies and puddings from anybody they met carrying of them in the streets; with a multitude of other impertinences so ridiculous in themselves, and troublesome to all sorts of people, that they were soon dropt, after they had been sufficiently laughed at. (*Bishop Burnet's History*, 4.182)

Mary even tried by fiat to suppress vice in the army and navy, though without much success. Notwithstanding that some of them were excessive, the result of all Mary's endeavours, according to the dissenters who presented William with an address of condolence on her death, was 'that the Court, that is usually the centre of vanity and voluptuousness became virtuous by the impression of her example' (Bates, 25).

Death and mourning

Mary died on 28 December 1694. She had not been well since 24 November, when she was present at a service conducted by Archbishop Tillotson at which he had collapsed with a stroke from which he never recovered, dying a few days later. The first signs of Mary's fatal illness appeared on 19 December. She shook these off initially, so that it was hoped she only suffered from measles. But by the end of Christmas day it became clear that she was suffering from the most virulent smallpox. Archbishop Tenison felt duty bound to inform her that she was dying, for which she thanked him, since 'she had nothing then to do, but to look up to God and submit to his will' (*Bishop Burnet's History*,

Jacobites insisted that Mary's death was a judgment of God
upon the queen. One pamphleteer pointed out that she died
in the same month that her father had endured an unnatural rebellion, while she was cut off in her prime—she was
only thirty-two—according to the punishment threatened
to breakers of the fifth commandment. A Jacobite 'Epitaph'
appeared:

> Here ends, notwithstanding her specious pretences,
> The undutiful child of the kindest of princes.
> Well here let her lie, for by this time she knows,
> What it is such a father and king to depose.
> (Strickland, 6.130)

Mary's admirers turned the tables on her detractors,
claiming that her death was a judgment on the nation for
its sins. 'We have just cause to fear our sins have hastened
her death' preached the duke of Newcastle's chaplain:

> God in his goodness sent us such a princess as was both a
> patroness and an example of goodness: a glass by which
> this crooked age might have rectified itself; and seeing he
> has waited divers years, and found no amendment, what
> was it but just to take the mirror from us? What should
> they do with a light who will not walk by it? (Pead, 19)

'Natural causes had their share in this evil', conceded Archbishop Tenison, 'but it was the immorality, the sin of the
nation which hastened it as a judgment' (Tenison, 26).

Mary's body was embalmed the day she died, a necessary precaution in view of the putrescent effects of smallpox. It took from 28 December 1694 to 21 February 1695 to prepare for her lying-in-state, which took place from noon until five o'clock every day until 5 March. Although Mary herself had privately expressed the wish for a simple funeral, she was then buried with elaborate ceremony in Westminster Abbey. Sir Christopher Wren supervised the construction of a railed walk from the Banqueting House to the abbey, along which the funeral procession made its way in a blinding snowstorm. For the first time in English history the coffin of a monarch was accompanied by members of both houses of parliament. Although normally they were dissolved by the death of a king or queen regnant, William's surviving her as sole monarch created a unique situation. Consequently Mary's funeral procession was the largest ever held for an English monarch. The mourners entered the abbey to the solemn strains of Henry Purcell's specially composed funeral anthem. The casket was laid under a catafalque designed by Wren, while the archbishop of Canterbury preached a sermon, and then it was lowered into the tomb. A wax effigy of the dead queen was placed on display in the abbey, so that Mary's image would be perpetuated beyond the grave. She herself had not wanted her funeral to be expensive, but the total cost came to about £100,000.

The queen remembered

Mary's reputation was fiercely disputed between Jacobites and Williamites. A Jacobite epitaph summed up the view of James's supporters:

Between vice and virtue she parted her life,
She was too bad a daughter and too good a wife.
(Strickland, 6.130)

On the other hand John Somers, the whig leader, stated in parliament 'I believe her the best woman in the world' (Cobbett, *Parliamentary History*, 5.631). Mary generated these contrary responses in her subjects. The public image she projected could foster both. Her behaviour on taking over Whitehall Palace in 1689 certainly seemed unfeeling in a daughter, while her toleration of William's infidelity did seem to be beyond the call of duty, even given the lax court morals of the age. At the same time her piety struck many observers as being sincere. 'If any person came to visit her in the morning before she pour'd forth her prayers', observed one admirer, 'she sent them back with this expression *That she was first to serve the King of Kings*' (*The Royal Diary*, 2).

Her private memoirs, letters, and meditations, however, leave little doubt that the eulogists were nearer the truth than the detractors. The survival of these papers, some preserved in French, gives a rare insight into her private thoughts. They document a simple piety and devotion to the Church of England. Of course she was no saint, as she readily admitted to herself. Her treatment of her sister Anne could be called an unnecessary vendetta. Yet she clearly felt affection for her father until he forfeited it by countenancing the death of her husband. And, although their marriage got off to a rocky start, William and Mary did come to respect and even perhaps to love each other with the passage of the years. Certainly he was distraught at the onset of her fatal illness, risking infection from smallpox himself by insisting on ministering to her, and her death devastated him.

Mary was a passionate and intelligent woman, which made her sensitive to her position. She was very aware of the role which, in her view, she had been called upon by providence to play. And she played it well. Her actions at the time of the revolution of 1688 reconciled many Anglicans, who were uneasy about replacing James with William, to the new regime. She did not wish to rule as well as to reign, being more than content to let her husband exercise the executive authority. But, when called upon in his frequent absences to administer affairs, she showed that she was quite able to do so, and to stand up to the cynical and experienced politicians with whom she had to work.

Perhaps above all Mary was prepared for death. She read Charles Drelincourt's *Art of Dying Well* (its published title was *The Christian's Defence Against the Fears of Death*) seven times over. She often expressed indifference to dying, only wishing that she would die before William. She got her wish. And after the delirium in the first onset of her final illness, in which she raved alarmingly, she became perfectly composed and conscious of her fate. Mary had learned Drelincourt's lesson and died an exemplary death.

Sources for Mary

J. Dalrymple, *Memoirs of Great Britain and Ireland*, 2 vols. (1771–3) · Countess Bentinck, ed., *Lettres et mémoires de Marie, reine d'Angleterre* (1880) · B. Bathurst, ed., *Letters of two queens* (1924) · R. Doebner, *Memoirs of Mary, queen of England* (1886) · *Bishop Burnet's History of his own time*, ed. M. J.Routh, 2nd edn, 6 vols. (1833) · *The life and letters of Sir George Savile…first marquis of Halifax*, ed. H. C. Foxcroft, 2 vols. (1898) · *Memoirs of Thomas, earl of Ailesbury*, ed. W. E. Buckley, 2 vols., Roxburghe Club, 122 (1890) · *Report on the manuscripts of Allan George Finch*, 5 vols., Historical Manuscripts Commission, 71 (1913–2003), vols. 2, 4 · G. Burnet, *An essay on the memory of the late queen* (1695) · W. Bates, *A sermon preached upon the…death of…Queen Mary* (1695) · T. Tenison, *A sermon preached at the funeral of her late majesty Queen Mary* (1695) · D. Pead, *A practical discourse upon the death of our late gracious queen* (1695) · [P. de Laine], *The life of that incomparable Princess Mary* (1695) · *The royal diary: to which is prefixt the character of his Royal Consort Queen Mary II* (1705) · 'Diary of Dr Edward Lake…in the years 1677–8', ed. G. P. Elliott, *Camden miscellany, I*, Camden Society, 39 (1847) · G. de F. Lord and others, eds., *Poems on affairs of state: Augustan satirical verse, 1660–1714*, 7 vols. (1963–75), vol. 5 · W. Sherlock, *A sermon preached…December 30, 1694* (1694) · A. Strickland and [E. Strickland], *Lives of the queens of England*, new edn, 6 vols. (1901–4), vols. 5, 6 · E. Gregg, *Queen Anne* (1980) · R. P. Maccubbin and M. Hamilton-Phillips, eds., *The age of William III and Mary II: power,*

150 politics and patronage (1989) · L. Schwoerer, ed., *The revolution of 1688–1689: changing perspectives* (1992) · T. Claydon, *William III and the godly revolution* (1996) · *The correspondence of Henry Hyde, earl of Clarendon, and of his brother Laurence Hyde, earl of Rochester*, ed. S. W. Singer, 2 vols. (1828) · A. Fraser, *The weaker vessel: women in seventeenth century England* (1984) · M. Walker, *Ungrateful daughters. The Stuart princesses who stole their father's crown* (2002).

Index

Enjoy biography? Explore more than 55,000 life stories in the Oxford Dictionary of National Biography

The biographies in the 'Very Interesting People' series derive from the *Oxford Dictionary of National Biography*—available in 60 print volumes and online.

To find out about the lives of more than 55,000 people who shaped all aspects of Britain's past worldwide, visit the *Oxford DNB* website at **www.oxforddnb.com**.

There's lots to discover …

Read about remarkable people in all walks of life—not just the great and good, but those who left a mark, be they good, bad, or bizarre.

Browse through more than 10,000 portrait illustrations— the largest selection of national portraiture ever published.

Regular features on history in the news—with links to biographies—provide fascinating insights into topical events.

Get a life … by email

Why not sign up to receive the free *Oxford DNB* 'Life of the Day' by email? Entertaining, informative, and topical biographies delivered direct to your inbox—a great way to start the day.

Find out more at www.oxforddnb.com

'An intellectual wonderland for all scholars and enthusiasts'

Tristram Hunt, *The Times*

The finest scholarship on the greatest people...

Many leading biographers and scholars have contributed articles on the most influential figures in British history: for example, Paul Addison on Winston Churchill, Patrick Collinson on Elizabeth I, Lyndall Gordon on Virginia Woolf, Christopher Ricks on Alfred Tennyson, Frank Barlow on Thomas Becket, Fiona MacCarthy on William Morris, Roy Jenkins on Harold Wilson.

'Paul Addison's Churchill ... is a miniature masterpiece.'

Piers Brendon, *The Independent*

Every story fascinates...

The *Oxford DNB* contains stories of courage, malice, romance, dedication, ambition, and comedy, capturing the diversity and delights of human conduct. Discover the Irish bishop who was also an accomplished boomerang thrower, the historian who insisted on having 'Not Yours' inscribed on the inside of his hats, and the story of the philanthropist and friend of Dickens Angela Burdett-Coutts, who defied convention by proposing to the Duke of Wellington when he was seventy-seven and she was just thirty. He turned her down.

'Every story fascinates. The new ODNB will enrich your life, and the national life.'

Matthew Parris, *The Spectator*

www.oxforddnb.com

At 60,000 pages in 60 volumes, the *Oxford Dictionary of National Biography* is one of the largest single works ever printed in English.

The award-winning online edition of the *Oxford DNB* makes it easy to explore the dictionary with great speed and ease. It also provides regular updates of new lives and topical features.

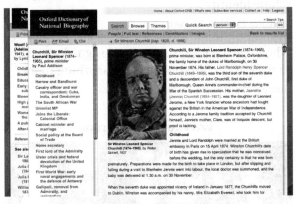

www.oxforddnb.com

The *Oxford Dictionary of National Biography* was created in partnership with the British Academy by scholars of international standing.

It was edited by the late Professor H. C. G. Matthew, Professor of Modern History, University of Oxford, and Professor Sir Brian Harrison, Professor of Modern History, University of Oxford, with the assistance of 14 consultant editors and 470 associate editors worldwide.

Dr Lawrence Goldman, Fellow and Tutor in Modern History, St Peter's College, Oxford, became editor in October 2004.

What readers say

'The *Oxford DNB* is a major work of reference, but it also contains some of the best gossip in the world.'

John Gross, *Sunday Telegraph*

'A fine genealogical research tool that allows you to explore family history, heredity, and even ethnic identity.'

Margaret Drabble, *Prospect*

'The huge website is superbly designed and easy to navigate. Who could ask for anything more?'

Humphrey Carpenter, *Sunday Times*

www.oxforddnb.com